WOMEN WITH ADHD

A Practical Guide to Break the Cycle of Chaos, Distraction, Shame and Stress of Living with ADHD. 150+ New Tips and Strategies to Embrace Neurodiversity, Change your Life & Thrive

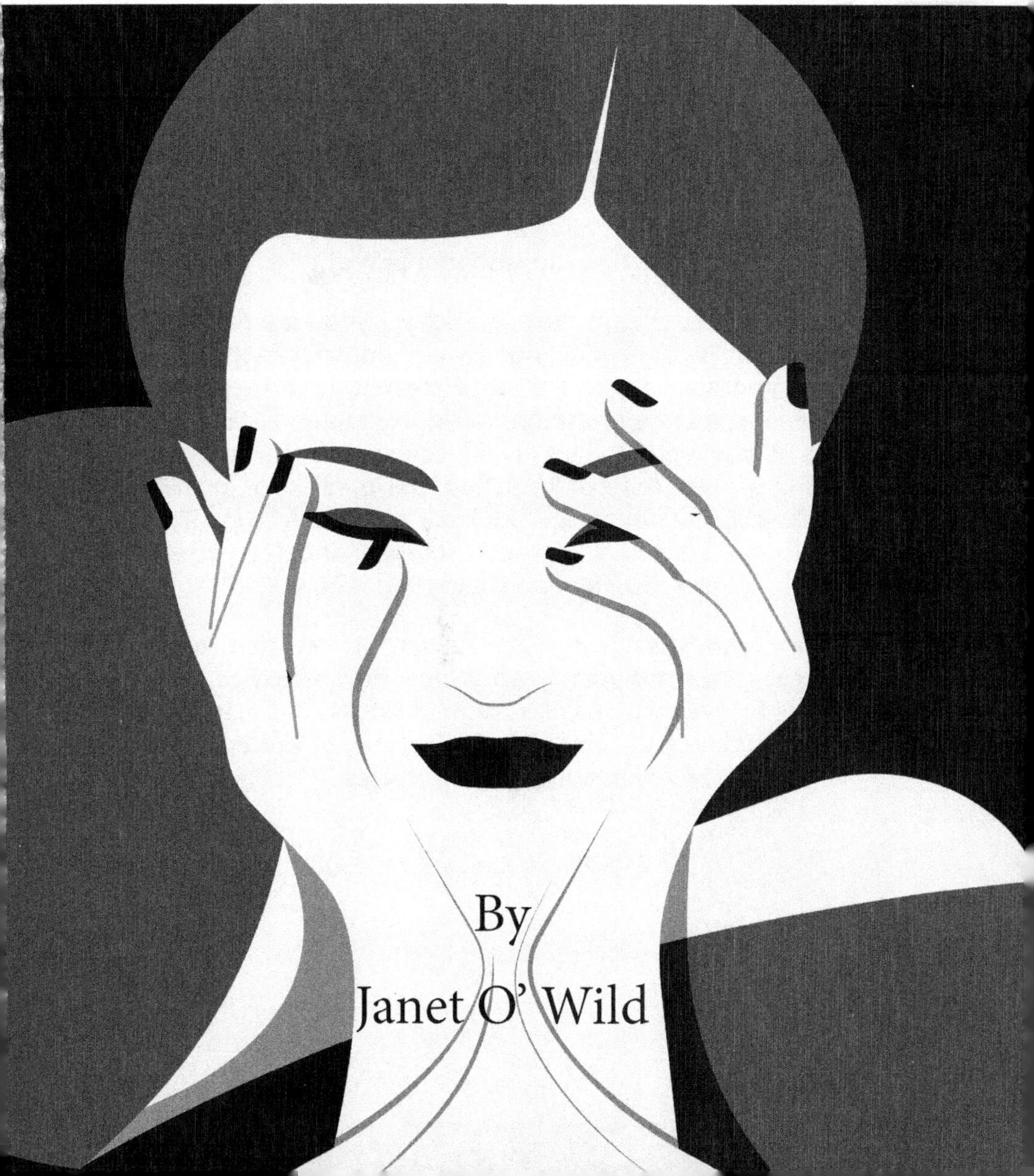

By
Janet O' Wild

© Copyright 2021 by Janet O' Wild - All rights reserved.

The content contained within this book may not be reproduced, duplicated, or transmitted without direct written permission from the author or the publisher. Under no circumstances will any blame or legal responsibility be held against the publisher or author for any damages, reparation, or monetary loss due to the information contained within this book. Either directly or indirectly.

Legal Notice: This book is copyright protected. This book is only for personal use. You cannot amend, distribute, sell, use, quote, or paraphrase any part, or the content within this book, without the consent of the author or publisher.

Disclaimer Notice: Please note the information contained within this document is for educational and entertainment purposes only. All effort has been executed to present accurate, up-to-date, and reliable, complete information. No warranties of any kind are declared or implied. Readers acknowledge that the author is not engaging in the rendering of legal, financial, medical, or professional advice. The content within this book has been derived from various sources. Please consult a licensed professional before attempting any techniques outlined in this book.

By reading this document, the reader agrees that under no circumstances is the author responsible for any losses, direct or indirect, which are incurred as a result of the use of the information contained within this document, including, but not limited to—errors, omissions, or inaccuracies.

TABLE OF CONTENTS

INTRODUCTION	**6**
Chapter 1: What is ADHD?	**8**
1.1 Types of ADHD	11
Other kinds of ADHD- Causes and Treatments:	13
Chapter 2: ADHD in Women and Girls	**16**
2.1 ADHD in Girls	16
2.2 Can ADHD Predispose You to Other Disorders?	18
2.3 ADHD In Women	19
2.4 Symptom Checklist of ADHD in Women	21
"Do you think you have ADHD"?	23
2.5 The responsibility of ADHD	25
Chapter 3: ADHD in the Various Phases of Women	**26**
3.1 Living with ADHD	27
3.2 Different Impacts of ADHD on Women	28
3.3 ADHD and Adolescence	29
3.4 Hormonal Effects on ADHD	30
3.5 ADHD and the Reproductive Years	31
3.6 ADHD and Childbirth	32
3.7 Like Mother, Like Child	33
3.8 Perimenopause Problems	36
3.9 ADHD and Menopause	37
3.10 Retirement with ADHD	37
Chapter 4: ADHD Comorbidities & Related Conditions	**41**
4.1 When ADHD Isn't the Only Problem – Comorbid Conditions	41
4.2 What Is Comorbidity?	43
4.3 Is It Just ADHD?	46
4.4 Type 2 Diabetes and ADHD	51
4.5 DESR and ADHD	54
Chapter 5: Intense Emotions and Negative Thoughts	**58**
5.1 7 Emotions That Throw You Off Balance	59

5.2 Break the Cycle of Shame   61
5.3 ADHD Challenges Don't Determine Who You Are   64
5.4 ADHD Brain Thinking   65
5.5 You're Stuck Because of These 10 Negative Thoughts.   68
5.6 15 Mindful Habits Your Brain Wants.   69
5.7 Getting Your Confidence Back   72
5.8 Rebuilding Your Self-Esteem after ADHD Diagnosis   74
5.9 Rejection Sensitive Dysphoria and ADHD   75
5.10 How to Live More Authentically with ADHD?   82

Chapter 6: Exercise and Healthy Eating   85
6.1 ADHD-friendly sports for women   86
6.2 Motivational tips to stay on track   88
6.3 Healthy Eating for ADHD Brains   90
6.4 Diet to Helps You Stay Focused   95
6.5 Natural Supplements and Vitamins to Treat ADHD   97

Chapter 7: Sleep & Mornings   100
7.1 9 Solutions to Sleep Deprivation for Individuals with ADHD   102
7.2 Have Difficulty Risen In The Morning?   105

Chapter 8: Anxiety and Stress   107
8.1 Anxiety and ADHD: Connections Symptoms and Coping Mechanisms   107
8.2 How Do You Handle Anxiety and Stress?   110
8.3 The 9 Stress-Relieving Points   112
8.4 7 ADHD Relaxation Tricks   115

Chapter 9: Mindfulness for ADHD   117
9.1 ADHD Symptom Relief with Mindfulness Meditation   119

Chapter 10: ADHD & Relationships   123
10.1 Friendships   124
10.2 Love & Sexuality   127
10.3 Parenting   130

Chapter 11: Home Organization   133
11.1 Clutter   134
11.2 Manage Your House   138

11.3 Meal Planning | 141

Chapter 12: Money & Budgets | 144
12.1 The Money-Saving Tips for People with ADHD | 147

Chapter 13: Getting Things Done | 151
13.1 Productivity Can Be Attained by Talking | 152
13.2 For those with ADHD Stuck on Tasks | 154
13.3 What to Do When You're Feeling Overwhelmed and Exhausted | 156
13.4 Daily Routine Tips That Work for Women with ADHD | 158
13.5 Productivity Advice for ADHD Brain | 161

Chapter 14: ADHD At Work | 164
14.1 16 Aspirational Jobs for Women with ADHD | 168

Chapter 15: Stop Losing Things | 169

Chapter 16: Save Your Focus | 172
12 Ways to Stay Focused Throughout the Day | 173

Chapter 17: Stop Procrastination | 177
Where Does My Procrastination Come From? | 177
17.1 Tips for breaking procrastination | 180

Chapter 18: How to prioritize | 182
Find out what's most important to you | 182

Chapter 19: Time Management | 184
19.1 9 Rules to Save Your Time | 187

Chapter 20: ADHD Therapies Overview | 190
20.1 9 Most Effective Therapies for Adults and Children with ADHD | 191
20.2 Best ADHD Treatments for Women | 195
20.3 Nine Innovative Options | 198

Chapter 21: ADHD Women FAQ | 201
21.1 Frequently Asked Questions for Women with ADHD | 201
21.2 Professionals' Answers to the Top Ten Questions about ADHD in Women | 206

Conclusion | 212

INTRODUCTION

Throughout my life, I've been disorganized, reckless, and unable to concentrate. Nonetheless, despite the adversity, I always felt that this was merely who I was, that those characteristics were part of my personality.

There were subjects in which I excelled at school, mainly when they covered themes in which I was already engaged outside of class. Nonetheless, I spent the majority of my school years suffering from a severe inability to focus. My mind would go off-topic, despite how hard I tried to concentrate. This resulted in dissatisfaction and rising disciplinary difficulties throughout the years, as I fell farther and further behind on my duties.

The school was challenging for me, but in many respects, my life got even tougher once I graduated. A curious aspect of ADHD is how a structured environment may make life simpler for the person with ADHD while simultaneously making it more intolerable for the person living with ADHD. At least a few subjects at school piqued my curiosity. In comparison, graduating from high school with limited qualifications landed me in a wide variety of jobs that absorbed little of my attention. As is the case with many undiagnosed people with ADHD, I struggled to maintain a full-time job.

Now I understand why a disproportionate number of entrepreneurs have ADHD. ADHD transforms you into an intellectual magpie, chasing after each bright object that crosses your path. I'd flutter from work to task and leap into new endeavors with boundless zeal and ingenuity. However, I frequently walked away, leaving everything unfinished.

In many respects, the little success I had via writing enabled me to disregard my ADHD thanks to the numerous coping mechanisms I had created over the years to cope with it. Because I had achieved some measure of success, there could not possibly be anything problematic with me. Or, if there was, it was irrelevant: I was doing OK, wasn't I?

However, I was still battling on the inside. When I gathered the willpower to sit down at my laptop and write, I could produce good work, but my capacity to do so was irregular and unpredictable. My technique for undergraduate essays had been chaotic: I'd write a few lines and then browse the internet for a while, wander about the room, speak with my housemates, and then return to my desk ten minutes later and attempt to pound out a few more words.

It was 2017 when I decided to talk to someone about it and found out it was what I suspected my problem was. ADHD. I had done some research and believed I was an egregiously obvious case of this disorder. While I recognize that it's unwise to delegate medical inquiries to Google, looking at ADHD symptoms was like flipping through a personal checklist. The one absent thing - which may explain why my ADHD was overlooked as a child - was physical hyperactivity. My hyperactivity was primarily mental.

It's been about 4 years since diagnosis, and a lot has changed since then; my life has been steadily improving, and it's time to share with you what has made this transformation possible.

"How do I overcome the difficulties of living with ADHD?"

This book is a compilation of all the techniques and strategies I used and still use to deal with ADHD in every area of my life.

CHAPTER 1: WHAT IS ADHD?

ADHD, alternatively referred to as attention-deficit disorder, is a behavioral disorder typically diagnosed in childhood. It is characterized by impulsivity, inattention, and, in some circumstances, hyperactivity. These symptoms usually coexist; however, one may manifest without the other (s).

When hyperactivity is present, it often manifests itself by the age of seven or sometimes in very young preschoolers. Inattention or attention deficiency may not become apparent until a youngster is exposed to elementary school demands.

An alarming truth is the fact that a large percentage of girls with untreated ADHD grow up "too talkative," "spaced out," and "disorganized." Despite their parents and professors recognizing these young women's intelligence and capability, they may lag academically; in adulthood, they continue to suffer due to growing obligations and shifting positions.

Among the possible signs of childhood ADD/ADHD are the following:

- Incessant fidgeting or movement
- Interfering with others
- Difficulty with play with peers
- Inability to listen
- Susceptible to distraction
- Unable to complete one job before beginning another
- Impulsivity

An adult with ADD/ADHD is equivalent to an untreated child before maturity. Adults with ADD/ADHD are often diagnosed because of difficulties they experience at work or in their personal and social relationships and may exhibit the following symptoms:

- Constant tardiness
- Susceptible to distraction
- Excessive emotional outbursts
- Disorganization
- Inattention on topics of interest
- Inability to concentrate on tasks they find tedious
- Relationship difficulties
- Workplace conflicts
- Have difficulty initiating difficult jobs
- Difficulties with prioritization
- Difficulty meeting deadlines

Additionally, ADD/ADHD might manifest differently in women than in men. Men, according to studies, externalize their symptoms, making them more straightforward to notice and diagnose. On the other hand, women frequently internalize many of their symptoms, making it more challenging to obtain a diagnosis and the necessary care. Among the symptoms that women with ADD/ADHD may exhibit are the following:

- Inability to organize
- Distractibility
- Victims of continuous forgetfulness
- High susceptibility to stress and anxiety
- Low self-esteem and self-confidence
- Hypersensitivity to stimuli
- Difficulty with time management
- Difficulty in managing the home
- Difficulty in interpersonal relationships
- Difficulty on workplace

1.1 TYPES OF ADHD

Because everyone is unique, it is typical for two people to experience the same signs differently. These behaviors are frequently observed to be distinct in males and girls; boys may be perceived as more hyperactive, whereas girls may be perceived as being more inattentive.

There are three primary forms of ADHD:

1. ADHD Distractible and Inattentive Type:
A high degree of distraction and low levels of hyperactivity are the hallmarks of this type of ADHD.

If you have this ADHD pattern, you may show more inattention than impulsivity or hyperactivity. You may occasionally struggle with hyperactive behavior; this is not the main symptom of inattentive ADHD.

Frequently, women who exhibit inattentive behavior:

- They are prone to overlook details and become easily distracted
- Soon become bored
- Have difficulty concentrating on a single task
- Have trouble organizing their thoughts and acquiring new knowledge
- Misplace papers, pencils, or other necessary items for completing a task
- Do not appear to listen
- Saunter and look to be daydreaming
- Process information at a slower rate and with less precision than others
- Have difficulty following instructions

2. ADHD, Hyperactive or Impulsive Type:

This form of ADHD is defined by impulsivity and hyperactivity. Women of this kind may exhibit indicators of inattention, but they are less noticeable than the other symptoms.

Impulsive or hyperactive women frequently:

- Fidget, wriggle or feel restless
- Find it challenging to sit still
- Speak non-stop
- Interact with and play with items at every time
- They annoyed in calm activities
- Are perpetually "on the move"
- They are easily irritable
- Misbehave and are oblivious to the consequences of their actions
- Stutter responses and make improper statements

3. ADHD, Combo-Type.

The most prevalent form of ADHD. It's marked by hyperactive and impulsive behaviors, lack of attention, and distractibility. The National Institute of Mental Health has revealed that most children have combo-type ADHD; the hyperactivity is the most prevalent symptom among preschool-aged children.

If you have the mixture type, your symptoms do not fall neatly into the categories of inattention or hyperactive-impulsive conduct. Rather than that, a mixture of symptoms from both is manifested.

Whether they have ADHD or not, most women exhibit some level of impulsive conduct. However, in females with ADHD, it's more evident, manifests itself more frequently, and impairs your ability to perform at work, school, home, and in social environments.

OTHER KINDS OF ADHD- CAUSES AND TREATMENTS:

1. Classic ADD
Symptoms: inattention, distractibility, disorganization, and impulsive behavior. At repose, the brain usually operates; during concentrated tasks, the brain works less efficiently.

Cause: Dopamine deficit; reduced blood supply to the prefrontal cortex, cerebellum, and basal ganglia, all of which contribute to dopamine production.

Treatment: Stimulant drugs such as Ritalin, Adderall, Vyvanse, or Concerta, or stimulant supplements such as ginseng, green tea, Rhodiola, and the amino acid L-tyrosine, which is a precursor to dopamine; increased physical activity; fish oil with a higher EPA to DHA ratio.

2. Over-Focused-ADHD
Symptoms: Difficulty maintaining attention, transitioning from thought to thought or task to task; becoming trapped in negative thinking or actions.

Cause: Deficiencies in dopamine and serotonin; hyperactivity

Treatment: Supplements such as L-tryptophan, 5-HTP, alternatively, antidepressants such as Effexor, Cymbalta, or Pristiq; avoid a high-sugar diet, which may stimulate bad behavior.

3. Inattentive-ADHD
Symptoms: Inattention, distractibility, disorganization, procrastination, daydreaming, and introversion; neither hyperactive nor impulsive; affects girls more than boys.

Cause: Dopamine insufficiency; decreased prefrontal cortex activation.

Treatment: stimulant drugs such as Adderall, Vyvanse, or

Concerta, and stimulating supplements such as the amino acid L-tyrosine; a high-protein, low-carbohydrate diet; and regular exercise.

4. Temporal-Lobe-ADHD

Symptoms: Classic ADD symptoms, as memory, learning, and behavioral difficulties, such as impulsivity, aggressiveness, and mild paranoia.

Cause: Temporal lobe abnormalities; reduced prefrontal cortex activation.

Treatment: GABA (gamma-aminobutyric acid) is used to calm neural activity and prevent nerve cells from overfiring or firing irregularly; magnesium is used to alleviate anxiety and irritability; anticonvulsant medications are used to stabilize mood; ginkgo or vinpocetine is used to alleviate learning and memory problems.

5. Ring-of-Fire-ADHD

Symptoms: hypersensitivity to noise, light, and touch; episodes of cruel, vicious behavior; unpredictable behavior; rapid speech; and worry and fearfulness.

Cause: A ring of hyperactivity encircling the brain is the cause. The brain as a whole is hyperactive, with excessive activity in the cerebral cortex.

Treatment: Stimulants alone may exacerbate symptoms. Begin with a diet of elimination. If an allergy is suspected, GABA and serotonin levels are increased using supplements such as 5-HTP, GABA, and L-tyrosine, as well as medicine, if necessary. Start with the blood pressure meds like guanfacine, clonidine, and anticonvulsants, which help to calm general hyperactivity.

6. Limbic-ADHD

Symptoms: Low energy, Moodiness, frequent feelings of powerlessness or chronic low self-esteem, and excessive guilt.

Cause: Excessive limbic brain activity (the mood control center).

Treatment: Supplements such as L-tyrosine, DL-phenylalanine (DLPA), SAMe (s-adenosylmethionine); antidepressants such as Imipramine or Wellbutrin; exercise; and dietary adjustments.

7. Anxious-ADHD

Symptoms: Anxiety and tension, physical stress symptoms such as headaches and stomachaches, a tendency to anticipate the worst and freeze up in stress-inducing circumstances, especially when being judged.

Causes: Basal ganglia are too active.

Treatment: Promoting relaxation and increasing GABA and dopamine levels. When used alone, ADD stimulants increase patients' anxiety by supplementing with various "calming" substances, including magnesium, relora, and L-theanine. Imipramine or Desipramine are tricyclic antidepressants that can be used to treat anxiety. Even Neurofeedback helps alleviate anxiety symptoms, mainly for relaxing the prefrontal brain.

Because symptoms alter over time, the type of ADHD you possess may also change. ADHD will be a life-long difficulty for you. However, medication, treatments, and therapies can help you live a better life.

CHAPTER 2: ADHD IN WOMEN AND GIRLS

Many girls with ADHD—most of whom exhibit symptoms of inattention—are not considered as much as the impulsive, hyperactive boys who exhibit typical ADHD behavior. Recognizing the misguided and misinterpreted symptoms of ADHD in girls and learning how to redress this unfair imbalance for you or your daughter is vital.

2.1 ADHD IN GIRLS

Understanding ADHD in girls

It is known that the distinctions between females and males are not only limited to the way their bodies evolve. They can also be observed in how their brains develop and grow; these variations can make it more challenging to determine if a girl has ADHD. ADHD is a brain condition characterized by inattention or impulsive behavior patterns that can hinder daily activities.

Because ADHD symptoms are unique to women, many go undiagnosed. This can prevent women from receiving the proper care that could significantly improve their lives. It is calculated that between 50% and 75% of ADHD incidences in women go undiagnosed.

Signs and symptoms of ADHD in girls

A girl with ADHD, especially the inattentive type, can look like this:

- distracted in class
- may show a sense of hilarity or wit, be reticent or disinterested

- friendless
- bites her nails or the skin around her cuticles
- tends to seek perfection in everything
- The following habits in girls may suggest ADHD because they:
- are constantly chattering, even when parents or teachers beg them to stop
- are frequently cry, even over small disappointments
- persistently interfere in the speech or activities of others
- have difficulty focusing attention
- daydream incessantly
- are untidy. Their bedroom, desk, and backpack are always disorganized
- are unable to complete assigned work

ADHD may also major impact girls if they exhibit the following symptoms:

- stress
- depression
- anxiety
- insufficient self-esteem

It is unknown why ADHD manifests differently in females; however, these differences make it more difficult to detect the condition in female life. Occasionally, parents or teachers recognize the symptoms but disregard them. Due to their diversity, they may be dismissed as immature behavior or assigned to another condition.

How Is ADHD Diagnosed?

ADHD in girls is frequently initially identified in the classroom. A teacher is more likely to bring up the potential of ADHD after observing a student's behavior in the school. When parents are informed of the concern, they are typically invited to meet with the school counselor and teacher to discuss the next measures.

These approaches may include both you and your child's teacher closely monitoring your child. Additionally, your child's counselor may conduct specific tests. These tests may include a review of a medical examination checklist and symptoms to rule out any other possible causes of the symptoms. Your child's counselor almost certainly wants to know the following:

- the degree to which the symptoms are severe
- the onset of symptoms
- the location of your child when they exhibit symptoms, such as at home or school

This will assist you and your child's teachers in determining the best course of action.

2.2 CAN ADHD PREDISPOSE YOU TO OTHER DISORDERS?

If ADHD is not properly identified, young girls may struggle to operate in everyday situations. Things could worsen if girls absorb this conduct and blame themselves. This can result in them being irritable with themselves. These issues can wreak havoc on their academic performance and mental health.

They may also face a decline in academics or a failure to sustain friendships if the ADHD is left untreated. This can result in a low sense of self-worth. Low self-esteem is associated with more serious problems, including anxiety, depression, and eating disorders.

According to recent studies, young females with ADHD are 3 to 4 times likelier to attempt suicide. Additionally, they are 2 or 3 times more prone to self-injury.

2.3 ADHD IN WOMEN

In females, ADHD is just as common as in males, and new evidence reveals that it causes even more emotional distress in the female gender. Despite advances in the management and therapy of ADHD, some health care providers may believe that the disorder primarily affects men rather than women and girls. There is also a greater likelihood for women with ADHD to be undiagnosed (or misdiagnosed) and receive inadequate treatment than men.

ADHD Differs in Women
Because of antiquated gender preconceptions, too many females with ADHD go untreated, leading them to feelings of hopelessness, shame, or depression. Although many professionals now detect and correctly diagnose ADHD, many women still do not have a professional diagnosis. This is a big obstacle in the way of effective treatment.

As we saw, ADHD manifests itself in three ways: inattention, hyperactivity/impulsivity, or a mix of two.

Men and boys are more likely to develop hyperactive/impulsive ADHD, which manifests as restlessness, always being on the go, disruptive, talkative, impulsive, impatient, and having mood swings.

On the other hand, women frequently demonstrate inattentive ADHD, making it difficult to concentrate, stay focused, be organized, and listen to and remember information.

Some of the inattentive ADHD traits, such as shyness or impulsivity, are often misdiagnosed and seen as personality traits.

Why Women's ADHD Symptoms Are Frequently Excused

In girls, ADHD symptoms are often considered as character features rather than as indicators of a disorder. For instance, a female may be labeled as enigmatic, forgetful, or chatty. Later in adulthood, a woman may seek therapy for her problems but is labeled with depression or anxiety.

The good news is that knowledge of ADHD symptoms in women is growing, which means that more women can seek help.

Women with ADHD frequently experience the same sensations of overload and exhaustion as males with ADHD. Psychological distress, low self-esteem, inadequacy sentiments, and chronic anxiety are all prevalent. Frequently, women with ADHD feel out of control or in turmoil, and daily activities may appear incredibly large.

Our culture often expects women to take on the role of caregiver. But if ADHD circumstances make women feel helpless with difficulty organizing and preparing for anything, caring for others may seem virtually impossible. In addition, this cultural pressure can exacerbate a woman's feelings of insecurity.

2.4 SYMPTOM CHECKLIST OF ADHD IN WOMEN

Women with ADHD are frequently misdiagnosed. Too many females grew up being labeled as lazy, self-centered, spacey, or stupid due to their symptoms being overlooked or discarded. If you had an insult-filled childhood and low self-esteem, do these self-tests to determine whether you exhibit common ADD symptoms. Then, before seeking a diagnosis, share the results with your doctor.

How to recognize your ADHD

1. Do you find yourself unable to reach your goals because of a lack of time, money, or other?

2. Is it hard to concentrate while in a crowded store, at work, or at a party? Do you feel like you'll never be able to block out the noises and sights that other people don't see or hear?

3. Throughout the day, do you find yourself shutting down because you've been offended? What happens when you feel emotionally overwhelmed by someone else's judgment?

4. Don't invite anyone into your home because you are ashamed of the clutter?

5. How much time do you spend coping, seeking items, catching up on orders?

6. Is it a challenge for you to keep your bank account in the black?

7. Do you often feel like a couch potato or a tornado on a deregulated activity spectrum?

8. Do you feel out of control? Can't meet all the demands on your time?

9. Do you believe that your ideas are superior to those of others, but you cannot organize or implement them?

10.   Have you ever seen people your age and intellectual level walk right past you? If so, do you try to stay away from those folks?

11.   Do you wake up every day resolved to be more organized, but by the time you go to bed, you're already disorganized?

12.   Does tackling, being organized, or keeping it, all together take up all your energy, leaving you with no time for what you enjoy or relaxing?

13.   Are you pessimistic about achieving your full potential and achieving your objectives in life?

14.   Do you have no idea how other people maintain a regular schedule?

15.   Have you ever been accused of being self-centered because you don't send birthday cards or thank-you notes to people?

16.   "A slob," "spacey," etc., are terms that describe you? Do you ever feel like you overdo your behaviors?

"DO YOU THINK YOU HAVE ADHD"?

Do you procrastinate or put off starting a new critical project?
Never
Rarely
Often
Very Often

Do you find it difficult to accomplish most of your duties (such as a job or school assignments) because they are monotonous or boring?
Never
Rarely
Often
Very Often

Is it common for you to be agitated?
Never
Rarely
Often
Very Often

Do you have a hard time relaxing, or do you constantly feel on the go?
Never
Rarely
Often
Very Often

Do you frequently forget appointments or obligations that are extremely important to you?
Never
Rarely
Often
Very Often

Do you think it's hard to stay focused on what others say when they talk to you?
Never
Rarely
Often
Very Often

When there is a lot of activity or commotion around you, are you easily distracted (or unable to focus)?
Never
Rarely
Often
Very Often

Do you frequently lose (or can't seem to locate) things?
Never
Rarely
Often
Very Often

Do you avoid circumstances like standing in line at the supermarket when it is anticipated?
Never
Rarely
Often
Very Often

If most of your responses are Often or Very Often, you should seek the advice of a qualified specialist. Only a clinical evaluation will yield an accurate diagnosis.

2.5 THE RESPONSIBILITY OF ADHD

Life has been a mess for many (if not most) women with ADHD since birth. The neurotypical world recognizes attention deficit hyperactivity disorder in children and teens. Yet, adults—especially adult women—are given significantly less attention because of society's harsh expectations and unspoken personal difficulties, further burdening them.

We have been hearing criticism and feeling condemned since we were children. Instead of deflecting blame onto others ("It was my friend's fault we got in trouble, not mine" or "My boss is cruel, that's why he fired me"), women with ADHD are taught to take it personally. We feel guilty about everything that goes wrong with us or others around us.

As they become adults, women take on new responsibilities, such as mother, wife, caregiver, waitress, cook, teacher or nursing assistant, etc. We with ADHD are used to wondering, "Why can't I do this? There's something wrong with me because everyone else is able to do it!"

Unfortunately, for women with ADHD, many difficulties arise that other women do not experience; ADHD leaves a mark on their self-esteem. They often feel like failed women, while the whole world expects them to take on their responsibilities without complaint.

CHAPTER 3: ADHD IN THE VARIOUS PHASES OF WOMEN

Women do not have ADHD, do they?! Yes, indeed, adult females are the quickest increasing demographic for ADHD diagnosis. In other terms, you are not the only one in your conflicted emotions, in your recovery, or your opportunity for a new beginning.

3.1 LIVING WITH ADHD

Women diagnosed with ADHD as adults often had their 'Aha!' moment once their kid was diagnosed. Suddenly, you begin to see yourself and your life's challenges reflected in the diagnosis. You've always known something was wrong, and now that you've learned about the symptoms of this disorder, you believe you have ADHD. What are the next steps?

Develop Expertise
Is your life a constant struggle? Are you constantly dissatisfied and frustrated? The first stage in your ADHD quest is to establish a diagnosis.

Accurate diagnosis. Begin by becoming as knowledgeable as possible about adult ADHD, to the extent where you know more about the problem than your doctor does. Discuss associated conditions with him/her—such as anxiety, mental disorders, or sleep difficulties—to help you understand symptoms that were previously neglected or misdiagnosed.

Embrace your Grief
If the first step is the diagnosis, the second step is to begin viewing your life in two main phases: pre-and post-diagnosis. After your doctor diagnoses you with ADHD, a new chapter begins! However, you must first obtain peace during the pre-diagnosis period, so be careful to address your feelings. You require time to mourn and reconcile with the knowledge. Only until you've processed your emotions, you can move forth with a clear understanding of your new life.

From adolescence to menopause, ADHD takes on varied appearances in women.
ADHD can manifest itself in various ways throughout your daily life. If you have these symptoms while at work or school, they may be exacerbated or more pronounced. You may find yourself exerting a great deal of effort to appear

"normal."

You might have been labeled a tomboy as a child because of your boundless energy and need to keep yourself busy. When you're an adult, making and keeping friends might be challenging because of the complexities of social norms. People might say you're the most talkative person they've ever met because of it.

While you may be outgoing, attending gatherings and other social occasions may make you uncomfortable and shy. Unless you're speaking or the subject is interesting to you, your attention tends to wander during conversations.

You may wish you could be a better friend, lover, or mother and that you could accomplish the things other people achieve. Say you'd like to bake cookies, remember birthdays, and be on time for a date.

People may assume you don't care if you can't do what society expects of you.

It's exhausting to be at work. Your office desk is overflowing with paperwork. Even when you put in a lot of effort to keep it clean, the order lasts a few days. It's difficult to concentrate when there's so much noise and people around. The only moment you can work efficiently is when everyone has left, and it is quiet, so you can stay late or come in early.

3.2 DIFFERENT IMPACTS OF ADHD ON WOMEN

Do you notice that your ADHD symptoms worsen around specific times of the month? Does your thought process a touch hazy a week before your period? Are you organized and productive in the middle of the cycle?

Doctors have discovered a link between ADHD symptoms and hormones, not only seasonally but throughout a woman's lifetime.

Women with ADHD who were not diagnosed as youngsters are diagnosed at an average age of 35 to 39 years old. Girls and women were frequently misidentified as having a mood condition or an anxiety disorder before that period. Even if these are subsequent disorders, curing them does not address the underlying issue of ADHD.

Doctors rarely consider hormonal variations when diagnosing women and girls with ADHD and creating a treatment strategy. On the other hand, professionals are discovering more about the links between ADHD and hormones. From puberty to menopause, we detail six stages in a woman's life, explain what's going on hormonally, and suggest techniques to control symptoms.

3.3 ADHD AND ADOLESCENCE

Sarah, one of my friends, was diagnosed with inattentive ADHD when she was 12 years old. She was prescribed a small amount of Adderall and performed admirably in school. Sarah's life altered when she turned 14 and started ninth grade. The influx of hormones brought on by puberty, along with the pressures of high school, was challenging to bear. She was late for class, forgot her textbooks at home, and spent 3 hours on homework assignments before forgetting to give them in. It is unknown if her issues were from increased ADHD, hormonal fluctuations, switching classrooms, dealing with six different professors, or a mix of these factors.

Sarah's doctor informed her mother that their ADHD medication is metabolized more quickly as girls reach puberty. As a result, he upped Sarah's dose. The doctor experimented with different drugs at various dosages over the next three years.

The physicians withdrew the medications since the greater doses of medication led Sarah to lose weight and didn't seem to assist her.

Sarah, now 17, discovered a technique to manage her symptoms through trial and error: a small everyday dose of fish oil and Metadate pills. In the last year, she hasn't missed a single school assignment.

She's considerably pleased now that she's enrolled in more rigorous high school classes. And now that she's a little older, she's not afraid to discuss what's going on with her body. 'Are you getting your period?' she asks her mother when she becomes irritated, cranky, or distracted during those 1 or 2 two days of the month. If she responds positively, she knows she'll have to give her some leeway.

3.4 HORMONAL EFFECTS ON ADHD

Girls with ADHD, who usually enter puberty between the ages of nine and eleven and receive their periods between eleven and fourteen, are particularly affected by the "raging hormones" that can contribute to rebellion and dangerous conduct in teenagers.

According to research, females with ADHD in their early teenage years have more academic challenges, more aggressive behavior, earlier indicators of substance-related issues, and higher rates of despair than females who don't have the disorder. Unlike teen boys with ADHD, who are more likely to act out, teenage girls with ADHD are more likely to internalize their issues. This makes it simpler to disregard their difficulties.

ADHD drugs may become less effective due to hormonal changes throughout puberty, notably greater levels of estrogen and progesterone. Estrogen has been proven to improve a woman's responsiveness to amphetamine medicines. However, this impact may be lessened when progesterone is present.

Solutions: With your daughter's doctor, discuss various medications—or changing dosages of present medicines. Be patient as you discover what works best for you. Time management and organizing skills can be improved with behavioral methods.

Identify your daughter's assets and emphasize them during her menstrual cycle's roughest periods. Professors and other adults in a girl's life frequently focus solely on her flaws.

Encourage your daughter to finish schoolwork ahead of time if she observes her ADHD symptoms getting worse at particular times of the month. Make her study for a significant test or complete a paper a week before the deadline.

If your daughter becomes irritable or snippy, be patient with her. Rather than ranting, propose that she take a break. You'll be teaching her how to manage her time.

3.5 ADHD AND THE REPRODUCTIVE YEARS

As we know, from the first day of your period, the average menstrual cycle lasts roughly 28 days. During the follicular phase, which lasts two weeks, estrogen levels slowly climb while progesterone remains low.

Estrogen stimulates the release of serotonin and dopamine, two feel-good neurotransmitters in the brain. Studies show that for women with ADHD, the 1st two weeks of the cycle go more quickly than the 2nd two weeks when progesterone levels climb. Progesterone reduces the positive effects of estrogen on the brain during the 3rd and 4th weeks, known as the luteal phase, potentially lowering the efficacy of stimulant drugs.

Premenstrual syndrome (PMS) is more severe in women with ADHD than in women without the disorder. "In women with ADHD, feelings of melancholy and worry tend to worsen around this time." What's the good news? ADHD treatment can also help with PMS symptoms.

Solutions: Keep a three-month journal of your ADHD symptoms, noting when they appear and worsen during your menstrual cycle, and try to spot a pattern. Some women only suffer troubles one or two days a month, the week before their menstruation start. During the luteal period, the symptoms of ADHD in other women get worse for around 10 days.

Medication may be of assistance. Many women find that taking a low-dose anti-anxiety or antidepressant medicine a day or two before their period helps them manage their emotional ups and downs. Others find that modestly increasing their ADHD medication a few days prior makes them feel in control. Oral contraceptives help many women with ADHD symptoms by reducing hormonal fluctuations. Three weeks of estrogen-only pills, followed by one week of progesterone-only pills, appears to be particularly beneficial.

3.6 ADHD AND CHILDBIRTH

During pregnancy, almost all hormone levels alter because the placenta generates hormones and stimulates other glands, such as the adrenals and thyroid, to create additional hormones. Moms-to-be with ADHD face exhaustion, mood swings, and worry as hormone levels increase in the initial months of pregnancy. Many women with ADHD report feeling better when their estrogen levels rise as their pregnancy continues.

According to certain studies, panic disorder gets better with each pregnancy trimester before relapsing after delivery. ADHD probably follows a similar trend.

Hormone levels diminish in the weeks following childbirth. While hormonal fluctuations can cause mood swings and postpartum depression in all new mothers, women with ADHD may be especially susceptible to depression.

Solutions: During your pregnancy and while breastfeeding, you and your physician should re-evaluate your ADHD therapy. According to research, some medications used to treat attention deficit hyperactivity disorder have been linked to heart malformations and other issues in growing fetuses. If their mothers take stimulant medicine during nursing, their newborns may have substance misuse problems later in life.

Certain antidepressants appear to be good to consume throughout pregnancy and nursing, but you and your physician should talk about all of your choices and decide what's best for you. Many women find that stopping their ADHD meds allows them to function better due to the aforementioned hormonal changes.

Apart from medication, it's critical to get care both throughout pregnancy and post-pregnancy. Although hormone changes may help with symptoms of ADHD, the stress of the job, dealing with young children at home, pregnancy, and the worry of preparing for a new baby may outweigh any hormonal advantages.

3.7 LIKE MOTHER, LIKE CHILD

It's one thing to parent a child with ADHD; it's quite another to have the illness yourself. Even under ideal circumstances, being the mom of a kid with ADHD is not easy. However, when ADHD affects both mother and child, it becomes more complicated.

Over the years, I have collected testimonials from many women with ADHD, mothers frustrated with their inadequacy to meet their own needs, let alone those of their children. "How am I going to keep control of my kids when I can't even keep myself organized?" one of those asked me.

Moms with ADHD often struggle to supervise and discipline their children consistently. Additionally, their problem-solving abilities—the combination of instinct and rational cognition required to overcome daily obstacles—are considerably harmed.

The following five tips will assist such mothers in helping themselves—and their kids.

1. To properly care for your kid, you must first learn how to care for yourself.
A mother's natural propensity is to concentrate on her child's problems while ignoring her own. That appears to be the most compassionate thing to do. However, in the long run, it is counterproductive. It is impossible to meet your child's requirements effectively if your ADHD symptoms interfere. Therefore, if you are diagnosed with ADHD, the very first step is to seek proper therapy for you.

2. It's easier to find solutions to challenges if you seek the assistance of everybody in the family.
According to the studies, moms with ADHD are able to find as many answers to everyday problems as their friends without ADHD. On the other hand, their plans and strategies are less effective as they have more difficulty in implementing them. Typical family problem-solving meetings are a way to make sure your decisions are sound. If everyone in the family contributes suggestions to improve daily life, you will likely notice something you hadn't considered. Also, children are more likely to adhere to and abide by rules that involve

all family members.

3. Domestic rules are advantages – but only if they are followed daily.
Children often act better when they are aware of the expectations placed on them. The most effective strategy is to create a written document outlining the family rules and the penalties for violating them. Post this checklist on your refrigerator door or another conspicuous location to remind your children of their responsibilities—and to motivate yourself to be consistent in enforcing the rules.

4. Regular checks with your kids will keep you calm - and them out of trouble.
This is easily accomplished by setting a clock or timer that sounds once every thirty minutes. Stop what you're doing after you hear the alarm and investigate what your child is doing. It is relatively easy to monitor a child inside the home or playing in the backyard. But when your child is out of the house, you need to adapt. For example, you might inform your child that you will call him or her before and after sports practice, a friend's outing, or another activity.

5. Consult a psychiatrist or pediatric psychologist to help you with your child.
After your diagnosis, it's time to ask for a thorough evaluation, even for your child. If you think your child has more than just ADHD, a professional evaluation is needed to identify learning, motor, language, or executive function/organization difficulties. A clinical assessment may also be required to assess whether or not your child has depression, anxiety, OCD, anger attacks, or tics.

If you regularly adhere to these standards, life should go more smoothly. You won't become a more caring mother—you already are—but you'll feel much happier, less anxious, and more secure. Likewise, your children will.

3.8 PERIMENOPAUSE PROBLEMS

Menopause and perimenopause have little-known side effects. They may exacerbate your ADHD symptoms.

As we age, our lives become busier and more demanding, and our ADHD symptoms change as well. As women approach menopause, their hormone levels drop, making it more challenging to cope with ADHD symptoms. As you mentioned in your question, this worsening of symptoms may arise during perimenopause when estrogen levels decrease.

When estrogen levels fall, it's been shown that cognition declines. Word retrieval, memory, and other cognitive functions are difficult for women to master. Estrogen deficiency has been linked to depression and other mental health issues, and it is possible that ADHD medications and management measures will not be as effective as they once were due to hormonal shifts during this period.

What to do?
To begin, I recommend speaking with your doctor about these new issues. Consider if these issues have existed since your twenties or have gotten worse with the onset of menopause. Thyroid disease, allergies, etc., are all possibilities to rule out, in addition to the connection between ADHD and hormones.

If you've received the all-clear from your doctor, talk to him about your treatment options. A common mistake doctors make is to increase stimulant medicine in women whose hormonal shifts are causing the problems you've described.

Extra stress in your life could also be a factor in your problems. Is your manager putting greater demands on your time recently? Has anything else in your life been psychologically taxing on you?

If you're feeling stressed at work, try some of these tips for women. Identifying the difficulties is always the first step.

3.9 ADHD AND MENOPAUSE

By menopause, estrogen levels decrease by about 65%, a continuous reduction that begins ten or more years before menopause (perimenopause). Estrogen deficiency causes a decrease in serotonin and dopamine levels in the brain. Menopausal women frequently experience terrible moods, melancholy, irritability, fatigue, foggy thoughts, and memory lapses. These signs may be more prominent in women who have been diagnosed with ADHD.

Given the reduced cognitive abilities of their brains, it is more complicated for women with ADHD to focus and make sound decisions during this time in their lives.

Solutions: During menopause, hormone replacement treatment can help correct hormonal imbalances and improve cognitive performance. For many women, the optimal line of therapy is three to four months of estrogen alone, followed by ten days of progesterone.

Combining hormone replacement therapy and ADHD medications often results in significant improvement in symptoms.

3.10 RETIREMENT WITH ADHD

Adults with ADHD who were diagnosed in middle age, when the shift from childhood to adulthood was complicated, now have a similar need for knowledge to help them plan for a new, but no less significant, life change: retirement.

You might wonder, "What's so difficult about retirement?" While the difficulties faced by twenty-somethings with ADHD are apparent, it would be natural to think that the problems faced by older persons with ADHD will diminish as they near retirement. Managing ADHD can be easier if we think about

it in terms of:
- Strategies
- Structure
- Stress
- Support

To cope with independent living stress, young adults must acquire new life-management methods to deal with a fresh set of everyday life issues. As they encounter these obstacles, their stress levels rise, and the structure and support they receive from their parents diminishes.

After your full-time job ends, use these ideas to help you live a more rewarding life.
Anxiety and ADHD symptoms rise when stimulations are too high, putting the person into a state of "overwhelm." Instead, people with ADHD may experience sadness, lethargy, and boredom if their stimulation levels drop too low. Overeating, excessive TV viewing, and increased alcohol consumption are all symptoms of low levels of stimulation, which can lead to dangerous daily habits like binge eating.

The older adult is going behind the support and structure provided by the workplace, much like the young adult does when leaving home for the first time. Schedule, everyday productivity, and daily engagement with other adults all vanish overnight, leaving nothing but a sour taste in your mouth.

Just as a young adult is forced to learn new daily coping skills when they approach adulthood, so too is an older adult who has reached retirement age.

Creating structure, locating stimulating activities, and maintaining a sense of direction in retirement are all important. Here are some ideas to get you through this challenging time:

- Seek assistance with retirement planning. Don't just let things happen without doing anything about them. It's vital to have regular, healthy sleep patterns. Understand the dangers of sleeping excessively (often a symptom of stress) or developing sleep habits that include lengthy periods spent awake at night followed by long periods asleep during the day.

- Practicality is essential when it comes to eating healthy on a usual basis. Many people with ADD/ADHD eat poorly because they don't plan their meals in advance and instead rely on unhealthy snacks that contain little or no fruits or vegetables.

- Think about how you can better organize your days. Working part-time can be pretty fulfilling since it offers variety, structure, and a feeling of purpose, and the added financial benefit.

- Volunteer efforts could provide structure and stimulation. The finest volunteer activities are those that bring you out of the home regularly.

- Don't allow yourself to get socially isolated. Avoid this at all costs. Because adults with ADHD sometimes struggle with organization and planning, seek things that occur regularly and don't require much planning or initiative on your part.

- Actively seek out other people's help. Family members, friends, ADHD coaches, and professional organizers can all offer assistance.

- Don't fool yourself that just because you have "lots of time," you should start doing things you've always found difficult. As an illustration, paying bills, keeping records, and preparing a tax return.

- Consider joining a group or organization that will give you a structured environment to engage in the "things you've always wanted to do" if you can.

- Keep in mind that ADD/ADHD is a lifelong condition. Even if you're retired, you shouldn't disregard your ADD or ADHD symptoms. If you have ADHD, your final years may be the time to seek treatment and assistance.

Enjoy ADHD's "benefits." Curiosity is often one of ADHD's advantages, as it allows people with the disorder to be interested in a wide range of subjects and activities. Your retirement has allowed you to pursue your passions; build in the framework, support, and techniques to help you realize your long-term retirement goals, and you'll be golden!

CHAPTER 4: ADHD COMORBIDITIES & RELATED CONDITIONS

About 80% of people with ADHD have also been diagnosed with other disorders at some point in their lives. Learning problems, depression, anxiety, sensory processing disorders, and ODD are the most prevalent ADHD comorbidities.

4.1 WHEN ADHD ISN'T THE ONLY PROBLEM – COMORBID CONDITIONS

When a woman has only ADHD or ADD, treatment can be a game-changer for their life. Stimulants-especially when combined with behavior therapy, exercise, and diet-can help most adults with ADHD cope with their distraction, hyperactivity, and impulsive symptoms if treatment is calibrated to their specific needs.

Some women with ADHD, on the other hand, tend to have significant symptoms—such as depression, anxiety, defiance, and learning and organizational difficulties—even after their more severe ADHD symptoms have been resolved.

As an illustration: When a girl is diagnosed with ADHD, her doctor immediately prescribes a stimulant to treat the condition. With medical therapy, her parents observe some improvement in symptoms, but other difficulties persist. His teacher has also noticed an improvement in her attention span, but she still has trouble keeping up in class. Her irritability decreases, but she is still too stubborn. When ADHD is identified and treated but problems persist, it's a sign of another underlying disorder at play.

Half of all ADHD patients also have another condition.
Doctors used to think of attention deficit hyperactivity disorder (ADHD) as a separate illness. They were completely mistaken in their assumptions. Comorbidity is the term used to express the presence of two or more conditions in ADHD patients. Comorbidities of ADHD include the following:

- Anxiety
- Depression
- Learning disabilities
- Obsessive-compulsive disorder (OCD)
- Language disabilities
- Oppositional defiant disorder (ODD)
- Small or big motor difficulties
- Tic disorders
- Executive function difficulties
- Other neurological or psychological problems

Occasionally, these issues are "secondary" to ADHD, which means they're brought on by the stress of dealing with the condition's symptoms.

If a girl is chronically unfocused, she may experience anxiety at school. Disapproval and criticism from family members might make a lady depressed if she has untreated ADHD. Once ADHD symptoms are under control, subsequent problems usually go away.

When ADHD treatment fails to address additional disorders, they are typically signs of a "comorbid" disorder.

4.2 WHAT IS COMORBIDITY?

It's known as comorbid when two or more disorders or ailments occur simultaneously or consecutively. Different disorders coexist with ADHD or ADD, and these conditions are known as comorbid conditions. Comorbid conditions are sometimes referred to as coexisting, co-occurring, and multimorbidity, a less general term for numerous chronic diseases. Despite being treated for the underlying ailment (in this case, ADHD), they persist. Comorbid disorders necessitate a separate treatment regimen for each.

In addition to ADHD treatment, a woman with comorbid disorders may try behavioral therapy, coaching, and a second medication.

Three Common Categories of ADHD Comorbidity
All three of the comorbid disorders most typically identified with ADHD occur on a severity scale ranging from mild to high. Symptoms can range from more or less intense, depending on the underlying cause, which can be anything from genetics to environmental chemicals to prenatal trauma.

1- Cortical wiring problems
Structural abnormalities cause problems with cortical wiring in the cerebral cortex, the part of the brain responsible for advanced mental activities. The below are examples of cortical wiring issues:

- Executive function difficulties
- Language disabilities
- Learning disabilities
- Motor difficulties

Lifestyle improvements and academic adjustments are recommended to correct cortical wiring problems. They are not affected by medications.

2- Problems regulating emotions

Among the symptoms of inability to control one's emotions are:

- Anxiety disorders
- Panic attacks
- Obsessive-compulsive disorder (OCD)
- Depression
- Bipolar disorder
- Anger-control problems

Besides sadness and negative thoughts, depression can cause a variety of other symptoms as well. These include irritability, loss of interest in once pleasurable activities, sleep disturbances, decreased concentration, indecision and agitation, exhaustion, and inappropriate bursts of anger.

SSRIs (Selective serotonin inhibitors) are a class of drugs commonly used in conjunction with ADHD treatments to treat regulatory issues.

Bipolar disorder is a highly complex condition to treat because there are many different approaches. Working with a psychiatrist who knows how to dosage drugs combined with ADHD treatment is critical while dealing with this condition.

3- Tic disorders

Tic disorders are characterized by uncontrollable jerks of the entire body's muscles.

Verbal tics, which can range in severity from grunting to spontaneous blurting to, in sporadic cases, offensive words or phrases, are among the most common.

Frequent and involuntary movements such as eye blinking or jerking or repeated hand gestures are symptoms of Motor tics.

If numerous vocal and motor tics have been present for more than a year, they are symptoms of Tourette's syndrome.

How to Tell the Difference Between ADHD Comorbidity and ADHD Symptoms

The next stage is to assess if ADHD is the cause of the symptoms you or your child are experiencing or if those symptoms are indicative of a full-fledged comorbid disorder that necessitates further evaluation and therapy. There's no way to validate for sure without a litmus test. The best approach to making an alternative diagnosis is paying close attention to symptoms' onset and location.

- Secondary problems are those that appear only under specific conditions and begin at one particular moment. Was it just in third grade that your daughter began to have anxiety issues? She seems anxious when she's at school, but is she the same way at home? If this is the case, her anxiety is most likely a side effect of her ADHD rather than a legitimate comorbid condition. The same is true if your son's hostile behavior began just when he entered middle school.

- Comorbid conditions, on the other hand, are long-lasting and widespread. They can appear starting in early childhood, and they are present in all walks of life. As an example, they don't simply happen throughout the school day or working day; they're present on the weekends, during holidays, and during a party as well.

- Life adversities, such as stress, might set off ADHD-related mood swings. Bipolar mood swings can last for prolonged periods and appear to be unrelated to the outside environment. They are commonly passed down in families, much like ADHD.

4.3 IS IT JUST ADHD?

Antisocial personality disorder, depression, borderline personality disorder, and others that we will look at in this chapter are common comorbidities for individuals with ADHD. You need to consider the various comorbidities when choosing a medication regimen if you want to fully understand your mental health diagnosis and benefit from ADHD therapy.

An accurate mental health diagnosis relies heavily on the patient and their health professional discussing symptoms. You may believe that your doctor's job is all about drug treatments, but if you don't comprehend the diagnosis for yourself or a loved one, you may miss out on the therapy you require. You must effectively communicate with your therapist to learn as much as possible about how and why the diagnosis was determined.

A simple diagnosis of attention deficit disorder is not enough for many people with this condition. Many patients have symptoms that may have been caused by other disorders. This phenomenon is called "co-occurrence." Great! When you think everything is fine, you realize (or learn) that something else is wrong with you.

However, six disorders commonly co-occur with ADHD:
- Depression
- Antisocial personality disorder
- Generalized anxiety disorder
- Bipolar disorder
- Borderline personality disorder
- Autism spectrum disorder

Each of these issues can significantly impact how persons with ADHD are treated medically and therapeutically.

Bipolar Disorder and ADHD

Many symptoms of bipolar disorder are misdiagnosed as ADHD-combo because they match the signs of that ADHD pattern. Attention deficit disorder and hyperkinesia are symptoms common to both variants. Hyperkinesia is characterized by rapid eye movements (REM) and agitation.

Bipolar disorder symptoms, on the other hand, are more severe and include mood swings that last longer, low self-esteem, a sudden increase in agitation, and impulsive or self-destructive behaviors, as well as psychosis. Although patients with ADHD and co-occurring bipolar disorder are agitated or hyperactive during a depressive episode, this could be due to ADHD rather than bipolar disorder. This is the main reason why individuals may be misdiagnosed with unipolar depression instead of bipolar disorder.

Stimulants can produce mania when used to treat coexisting ADHD and bipolar disorder. It is far easier to tolerate and swiftly recover from stimulant-induced anxiety than it is from stimulant-induced obsession. These risks are known to prescribers. Hence ADHD symptoms in bipolar individuals may be undertreated.

In cases of ADHD and bipolar illness, it's essential to merge medication management and psychotherapy to stay up with and adapt to the emotional state, personality, and brain chemistry shifts that come with a significant mood problem. Clients, therapists, prescribers, and families all have a role to play in staying on top of these ebbs and flows. It is common to start patients with low dosages of a stimulant and gradually increase the dosage during treatment, seeing them weekly for medication review and therapy for the first month or two. If the dosage needs to be increased, it should be done slowly and carefully.

Anxiety and ADHD

ADD/ADHD and anxiety are often seen as the same side of the spectrum. People with anxiety tend to obsess over the smallest things, while those with ADHD tend to be less anxious. Treatment becomes more complicated when a person has both ADHD and anxiety simultaneously.

There are multiple factors to consider when dealing with ADHD coexisting with anxiety. When a patient is diagnosed with ADHD and anxiety, the first line of treatment is usually an SSRI or SNRI. These stimulants promote increased attention, ability to complete assigned tasks, organization, and a reduction in impulsivity, distraction, and conflicting interpersonal interactions. Factors that appear to limit the drug's effectiveness include the predominance of anxiety and depression in symptoms, organic injuries, and the presence of unfavorable socioeconomic and environmental conditions. All of these elements also lead back to the difficulty of defining this syndrome. Only after trying stimulants and witnessing this response can we know if a person has a mixed condition, in which case, stimulants are stopped briefly, and anxiety is treated first.

Anxiety can make it challenging for women to concentrate and manage daily activities, especially if they also have symptoms of ADHD. In some circumstances, their mind never stops racing, to the point of compulsions and obsessions. This level of anxiety makes it impossible to accomplish anything; in our terminology, it is referred to as "anxiety-primary." This is difficult to verify without a drug trial, even if we assume it exists. As long as an anti-anxiety medication also helps ADHD symptoms, this is the best route.

On the other hand, it's easy for a woman who suffers from anxiety to also have ADHD. Concerning disorders defined as "ADHD-primary" by physicians, people who suffer from them are continually nervous and anxious due to their ADHD symptoms. Their anxiety is reduced to a manageable level due to ADHD symptom treatment. Stimulant medicine is the fastest way to see if this occurs for a specific patient. If the level of anxiety decreases, we are there. This brings us back to the diagnosis of ADHD-anxiety, in which case treatment will often include an SNRI or SSRI.

Your doctor should be aware of and understand any changes in your symptomatology after the stimulant trial. Some women have started problems with stimulants and had poor results because the prescriber mistakenly overlooked the diagnosis of ADHD and excluded a valuable course of medication from the treatment plan. Instead, it is critical to complete treatment correctly. Being aware of the interactions between anxiety and ADHD will help you treat both effectively.

Depression and ADHD

Depression and ADHD are common co-occurring disorders. For example, they may show signs such as alternating irritability or sadness, low energy, changes in eating habits, sleep problems (too much or too little), feelings of worthlessness, and inappropriate guilt in addition to other negative feelings. Some women I interviewed even have suicidal thoughts or behaviors.

Depression is a typical side effect of ADHD. Women with ADHD may experience feelings of hopelessness and worthlessness due to the difficulty of managing ADHD symptoms, leading to diagnosed depression. Despite a thorough evaluation, the only method to reduce depression symptoms is to treat ADHD with medication and cognitive behavioral therapy. Often the results are encouraging.

In other circumstances, people initially respond well to stimulants, but their effects quickly wear off. Although stimulants help people feel better by giving them more energy and productivity, the improvement may be masked by coexisting depressive symptoms; moreover, its effectiveness applies only for the duration of the stimulant's action, usually eight to 12 hours. With this method, the treating physician can experiment with lower doses of stimulants, increasing the chance of successful treatment by addressing co-occurring depression and ADHD.

Women who have symptoms of depression may be successfully treated and then find that they still have difficulty in relationships, school, or their profession despite their improved mood. The woman feels a little better, but her condition has not improved stable, and lasting.

Occasionally, depression rather than ADHD is the root of the problem. These women are in such despair to the point of being unable to focus, organize, and cope positively with their lives.

Autism Spectrum Disorder and ADHD
There are various types of autism, ranging from mild to severe, making it difficult to compare one case to another. For individuals diagnosed with autism, the greatest difficulty is in communication and interaction with others. Affected individuals have limited interests and repetitive activities, and their functioning in school, work, and other areas of life that require human interaction is impaired.

Because ASD and ADHD have such a strong correlation, it is commonly understood as a differential diagnosis. It is definitely more difficult to address when a woman has both conditions. No medicine can make them more socially adept or disconnect them from their inner worlds, but stimulants can help people with ASD-ADD understand social norms and notice the nuances behind those rules. Mood swings and emotional breakdowns are also common in people with ASD-ADD, especially when overwhelmed by ordinary life events. Treatment for mood swings, like anxiety, may increase irritability rather than decrease it. One reason may be that some therapists do not distinguish between the two conditions that are more crucial and do not have a clear idea about the best dosage for that case.

People with autism spectrum disorders (ASD) may have mood dysregulation just like people with bipolar disorder and just like people with ADHD. In addition, stimulants taken individually are not effective for patients with ASD, so much so that clinicians have been advised to avoid their use. However, we have found that the right mix of mood stabilizers and stimulants helps these people function better. As a treatment for ASD-ADD, mood stabilizers and a cautious, careful, and well-integrated treatment strategy can be a valuable aid for those with this disorder.

4.4 TYPE 2 DIABETES AND ADHD

People with ADHD who typically have eating problems and dopamine-seeking behaviors make poor food choices, increasing their risk of developing type 2 diabetes.

There is an increase in the prevalence of type 2 diabetes in adults with ADHD.

34 million Americans have diabetes, and 95% of those have type 2 diabetes, according to the CDC (Center of Disease Control and Prevention). Failing to take charge of diabetes and treat it can lead to several major health problems, including kidney and heart disease, nerve damage, and over-the-limit blood pressure.

Type 2 diabetes is primarily diagnosed in people over the age of 45, but with rising rates of childhood obesity, now it is also diagnosed in many individuals in their 30s and 40s.

Having a sedentary lifestyle, being overweight, and having a family history of diabetes are factors that increase the risk of having high blood sugar and type 2 diabetes.

The body's ability to create insulin, a pancreatic hormone

that helps control type 2 diabetes, is damaged by persistently elevated blood sugar levels.

What you're eating habits say about your ADHD

The studies on the relationship between type 2 diabetes and ADHD are not conclusive but now make coexistence more likely given our current understanding of the neurological basis of ADHD.

Type 2 diabetes may be a prelude to eating disorders, which are 4 times more likely with the aggravation of ADHD; in fact, diets high in sugar and simple carbohydrates satisfy the ADHD brain's desire for dopamine stimulation. As if our brains are attracted to certain foods.

If people with ADHD fail to eat healthily, it's generally also due to weak executive function, which makes meal planning difficult. They forget to defrost lean meats for lunch, don't organize a healthy shopping list, and abandon physical activity.

Polycystic ovary syndrome, which can cause irregular menstruation or infertility, is also another link between type 2 diabetes and ADHD. The higher incidence of PCOS in ADHD women makes them more likely to develop diabetes.

To treat diabetes, you need to check your blood sugar levels before and after meals and keep track of what you eat. This is what you need to do every day, so type 2 diabetes treatment regimens can be complicated for ADHD patients to follow because they require regular monitoring.

Recognizing the symptoms of diabetes

For people with ADHD, it can be difficult to recognize the symptoms of diabetes. For many others, the signs and symptoms are obvious; they report increased thirst, decreased vision, fatigue, bruising, and skin wounds that take longer than usual to heal. Studies have shown a link between cognitive impairment and diabetes, particularly in the elderly; therefore, diabetes may complicate the diagnosis of ADHD later in life.

To reduce your risk of having type 2 diabetes, adopt the following healthy habits as soon as possible:

- **Check the nutrition facts of your meals.** Suppose you want to avoid eating too much sugar. In that case, check these entries in your food: HFCS, INN, dextrin, dextrose, maltodextrin, sucrose, molasses, and malt syrup are all names for the sweetener sucrose, which is included in all of these ingredients.

- **Reduce your weight.** Losing weight certainly positively impacts your blood sugar levels, cholesterol levels, and systolic blood pressure.

- **Opt for healthy food options when shopping for groceries.** Reduce your calorie and fat intake by eating high-fiber, low-fat foods. All children (and adults) should eat fewer (or avoid) highly processed foods, such as snacks, white bread, and sweets.

- **Increase your activity level.** Regular physical activity benefits your heart and brain. Doctors recommend 150 minutes of exercise each week - half an hour a day, five times a week. If that's not feasible for you, aim for two 15-minute periods of activity each day. Start each morning with 20 minutes of cardio or a light workout, then go for a walk after lunch.

4.5 DESR AND ADHD

DESR, or the inability to regulate one's emotions, is a critical aspect of ADHD that can have serious consequences. However, it is not one of the diagnostic criteria for the condition. There is some hope for the future now that a new study shows that emotional dysregulation significantly impacts the manifestation of ADHD and each patient's individual outcomes.

What is DESR?
DESR is a relatively new acronym used to explain the problem of impulsive emotions combined with difficulties with emotional self-regulation—concerns historically linked to ADHD.

Strong emotions can trigger misconduct, but it is possible to control them. On the other hand, emotional impulsivity (EI) is also a symptom of ADHD. It is characterized by impatience, low frustration tolerance, the tendency to anger, aggression, and other aversive responses, all related to the impulsive component of the disorder.

To understand the importance of EI and DESR in ADHD, one must recognize the significant role of emotional control problems in the onset and progression of the condition. People with ADD/ADHD are more likely to experience these problems. In the face of these difficulties, significant comorbid disorders are also expected to arise.

Although diagnoses for ADHD do not mention emotional dysregulation, most patients and professionals agree that it is a crucial aspect of the condition.

The ongoing emotional struggles are a multitude of compelling evidence from the clinical conceptualization of ADHD to neuroanatomical and psychological research that clearly shows that EI and DESR are critical components of

ADHD and should be incorporated into diagnostic criteria and treatment practices for the disorder.

ADHD, EI and DESR
An executive brain network known as the front-limbic circuit links ADHD to other disorders such as emotional dysregulation, motivation problems, and hyperactivity-impulsivity. The "hot" circuit is another name for this network's ability to regulate emotions and thoughts. Because of its importance in decision-making, I also call it the "why" circuit.

ADHD, on the other hand, can cause significant disruptions in the emotional regulation network.

EI and DESR, and the neuroanatomy of ADHD
ADHD-related brain networks and structures are inevitably linked to emotions. Therefore, EI and DESR are likely to develop and be part of the condition itself.

The executive circuitry of the brain, which includes the frontal lobe, anterior cingulate, ventral striatum, and amygdala, has been implicated in the development of ADHD. Emotions are formed in the amygdala and the larger limbic system to which it is connected, and the prefrontal cortex and adjacent structures attend to these produced emotions. Some of these brain areas also make up the emotional circuitry. We cannot think without feeling.

Comorbidities Underlying ADHD: EI and DESR for ODD
Here, it allows us to understand the basis of many comorbid conditions typically linked to ADHD, such as oppositional defiant disorder (ODD), and to confirm that emotional dysregulation and impulsive emotion problems are among the symptoms of ADHD.

Adults with ODD are consistently aggressive and irritating. They have the ability to get angry at the entire world daily and lose their temper for the most trivial reasons, often manifesting it with threatening verbal abuse. Adults with ODD are always defensive, and when someone tells them they have done something wrong, they react with real outbursts. The underlying reason is that they feel frustrated, rejected, misunderstood, and unloved.

The constant opposition to their duties makes it difficult for adults with ODD to hold down a job and maintain family and social relationships. By feeling misunderstood and unappreciated, they see themselves as victims and not the very cause of the pain within their relationships. All of these issues have a substantial impact on the likelihood of developing mental health problems.

ODD affects the emotional well-being of children as well because it promotes the risk of anxiety and depression in their 20s. The oppositional component of ODD enables antisocial behavior and conduct disorder in the school environment. The impulsive and emotional element of ODD is more likely to be found in family interactions.

ODD is more frequent in ADHD; thus, it is reasonable to believe that the emotional component of ODD is a byproduct of ADHD; that is, ADHD is likely to cause ODD. All comorbid conditions, especially anxiety disorders, are more likely to develop when ADHD remains untreated and emotions dysregulated. This theory explains why ADHD medications handle emotions and ODD so well, but only if ADHD is truly present as well.

EI and DESR: treatment considerations.
Understanding treatment outcomes is also aided by refocusing ADHD on emotions. As a result, we often see that ADHD medications have an impact on EI and DESR difficulties in ADHD patients, albeit in different ways. Stimulants seem to calm and even suppress the limbic system, causing patients to complain of feeling like a robot with bland feelings. Non-stimulants, such as atomoxetine, work on a different

area of the brain. They help upregulate the executive brain, allowing patients to better control their emotions. Prescribers can use a variety of medication combinations to provide individuals with more control over their ADHD symptoms, including emotional problems.

Other Treatment Considerations:

- ADHD medications can help with the secondary impairments of EI-DESR in major life activities.

- Adults with ADHD may benefit from cognitive-behavioral therapy (CBT) programs that target EI deficits and mindfulness-based techniques to help with emotional regulation, especially if they are on ADHD medications.

- Emotional dysregulation in children is best treated with medication and, to a lesser extent, with parental behavioral training programs that focus on reorganizing environments and relationships to avoid triggering high impulsive emotions.

- Clinicians should screen for ADHD in parents, not only through genetic inheritance but also treat their signs. In fact, parental therapy can play a positive role in emotional dysregulation in ADHD children by modeling poor emotional control and engaging in emotional interactions with the child.

In conclusion, EI-DESR is a historical idea of ADHD, and research in neuropsychology, neuroanatomy, and psychology has long linked ADHD to EI and DESR. This fundamental association could describe, at least to some extent, why the disorder puts patients at greater risk for mood disorders such as ODD, as well as other particular conditions that some patients manifest.

We can greatly improve diagnosis and treatment techniques by identifying the role of EI and DESR in ADHD.

CHAPTER 5: INTENSE EMOTIONS AND NEGATIVE THOUGHTS

Adults can have ADHD symptoms less visible than children's symptoms. Women with ADHD may experience restlessness, impulsivity, and difficulties paying focus; they may find it challenging to retain directions and information, prioritize projects, and complete work on schedule. Poor time management, chronic procrastination, low self-esteem, mood swings, and even troubles at work, school, and in relationships are all examples of these symptoms.

5.1 7 EMOTIONS THAT THROW YOU OFF BALANCE

Emotional instability is reported by over a third of adults and adolescents with ADHD as one of the most frustrating features of the disorder, despite the fact that emotions are not mentioned like diagnostic criteria.

Here are seven emotions that have the ability to knock us off our feet:

1. Emotional Flashes

Many persons with ADHD are completely surprised by their own feelings, especially when they shift so rapidly that there's no time to stop and ponder, reflect, or feel them. People act or express their feelings immediately and without thinking about the consequences when this occurs.

Flash anger is the most common abrupt emotion that gets ADHDers into trouble. "You go from zero to all in a second," said one patient. Some medications can alleviate this symptom and offer persons with ADHD the same 5 seconds as the rest of people to feel an emotion growing on and decide, "I really shouldn't express that."

2. Low Tolerance for Anger

Anger tolerance is relatively poor in ADHD people. Stressors might cause them to feel overly frustrated, and this can lead to behavioral problems. As a result, individuals cannot push aside unpleasant emotions and are instead overwhelmed by them, which becomes intolerable.

3. Anxiety perception

Often, persons with ADHD describe their feelings as "anxious," but what they really mean is something else. Physicians must first understand how and what the patient means when using specific terms.

4. Ignoring other people's emotions

People with ADHD can be overly involved and easily overwhelmed by events happening around them. Despite this, it is possible for them to appear insensitive to the feelings of others if they act cold or callous. Because of their lack of sensitivity or being overwhelmed, when they disengage from the demands of others, they may appear cruel or selfish.

5. Excessive Reaction/Easy Overwhelmed

Overreaction is a common problem for people with ADHD, as the emotional response often does not match the severity or nature of the trigger. People with ADHD may have difficulty understanding the difference between a serious threat and a minor inconvenience. More often than not, they overreact and need to be "talked down." Because of the characteristics of ADHD, most women are never comfortable. Their thoughts raced at a dizzying pace until they collapsed from exhaustion.

6. Afraid of Rejection

Women with ADHD have a high threshold for rejection and criticism. They are extremely sensitive people. People with ADHD may feel hopeless and demoralized if they try to get results by copying the successful methods used by those without ADHD, only to end up failing again because those methods don't work for them.

7. Guilt and Shame

Women with ADHD are constantly subjected to comparisons of their talents to those of neurotypical people, having a negative impact on their sense of self-worth and self-image.

These women with inattention/hyperactivity disorder (ADHD) struggle with mindfulness and social interactions, which leads them to self-exclusion. As a result, most women with ADHD believe they are somehow guilty of being inferior to others. In some circumstances, they may even think they are fundamentally flawed. "Damaged goods" is a term you'll hear often and refers to how someone with ADHD feels in general.

Because of the feelings of shame and guilt that come with it, people are more likely to miss out on favorable feedback. They are completely unaware of this, which is why they are much more sensitive to negative input. As a result, shame almost always takes precedence over all other feelings. Freud expressed it best when he observed, "The chief emotion is the shame." Because it is the only feeling that does not actively seek expression, it has the power to influence whether other emotions are noticed and therefore dealt with.

5.2 BREAK THE CYCLE OF SHAME

It is possible that showing signs of ADHD, such as forgetting appointments or being easily irritable, will get you a bad reputation. In addition, the cycle of ADHD symptoms and being constantly berated can encourage negative perceptions of yourself, leading to even greater, if unchecked, feelings of shame.

To make matters worse, if those around you don't understand ADHD or how its symptoms affect your daily life—or if your colleagues, supervisors, or friends don't give any concessions or understanding—you may feel lonely and stressed. In turn, these adverse reactions may induce further self-doubt, which can exacerbate your feelings of guilt.

ADHD-related stigma can also be a cause of embarrassment for you. Because you have been singled out for something you have no control over, this can also affect your mental condition.

According to a recent study, women with ADHD have much lower self-esteem than those without the disorder. In part, this is due to the constant unfavorable feedback they receive.

If you have a pessimistic attitude about your ADHD, you will feel embarrassed whenever others notice. Instead of feeling guilty about having ADHD, look at it as a gift and take joy in who you are as a person.

Feeling shame is a standard and understandable reaction to being criticized repeatedly. With or without ADHD, everyone will experience this feeling at some point in their lives. However, even if ADHD people often experience shame, it does not follow that you have the right to view yourself exclusively through a pessimistic prism.

You may be criticized for ADHD-related habits, but that doesn't mean your talents and character have been diminished as a result.

How to overcome shame
You may think that shame can always get the better of you. In reality, there are some great ways to help you manage these emotions of yours:

Find someone you can trust

If you've been dealing with shame, it's understandable that you're reluctant to openly tell those around you. If they don't approve of how you're acting, you may even worry that talking about it with them will simply add more shame. However, if you can share your experiences with someone you trust, that can give you a much-needed outlet.

So, if you have a friend who has shown compassion and trust, consider letting them know how much you appreciate them and confide in them. Talking to her can help alleviate that loneliness if you're feeling lonely. Spending time with friends and family who understand your struggles and don't make you feel guilty is a good thing for you and your self-esteem.

Feel compassion for yourself.

Shame may make you believe that your value as a human being is less than other women. Knowing the difference and being kind to yourself about your symptoms will help you combat shame.

In fact, one of the best actions you can take is to become aware of your limiting ideas about ADHD as soon as possible. It is much easier to change your perceptions if you know why you have them in the first place.

Investigate a group for people with ADD/ADHD.

Seeking out others who've been through the same thing as you can help you overcome feelings of humiliation and loneliness. Some organizations like Children and Adults with ADHD (CHADD) have support groups.

ADHD coaching is an additional alternative that can assist you in managing your symptoms and dealing with the associated negative emotions, such as shame.

Focus on the good things.

It's crucial to keep in mind the compliments you've received as a way to combat the criticism you've received. The feedback that focuses on your strengths can serve as a motivator and reassurance that you're improving and that you're deserving of respect and admiration.

A running record of your accomplishments (no matter how tiny) is an excellent tool to monitor your growth and return to it if you ever receive any negative criticism.

Recognize triggers.

If someone, something, or someplace makes you feel ashamed or feel horrible about yourself, you should consider it a trigger and address it.

No matter how much shame you are feeling, it is crucial to be aware of what might be causing it.

Being aware of the triggers will allow you to better address the underlying reasons why you feel guilty. If you feel guilty for interrupting someone in the middle of an argument, you can practice active listening and wait for the right time to join in.

To ease the tension that comes with finding and understanding a trigger, people with ADHD may request adjustments at work or alert a friend that they are having trouble managing time because of their ADHD symptoms.

5.3 ADHD CHALLENGES DON'T DETERMINE WHO YOU ARE

ADHD can make women believe they are mean and less loving. You may be one of those girls who grew up believing this. You may have felt safe and strong one day, but your negative thoughts and ADHD symptoms may have incapacitated you the next. You're still thinking about it, aren't you?

ADHD is not the only condition in which people experience shifting viewpoints and moods. Moments of clarity alternate with periods of illogical thinking in everyone. When we get angry at someone we care about, we feel terrible, but we don't feel bad when we are kind to a stranger. Even within the span of a single day, we are all unique.

However, these human discrepancies are unpleasant and disconcerting to the ADHD brain. Why? Women with ADHD have a tendency to see things in extremes, whether they are highly motivated or completely uninterested in doing something. Your mind feels compelled to take a stand. Our inclination to fluctuate and change from day to day keeps us in a state of static rather than deliberate thought and action.

Fortunately, becoming more aware of our thoughts and actions and leaving less room for gray in our worldview is something we can learn to do. The narrative we tell ourselves can be rewritten if we learn to recognize and accept the fact that we are more than the sum of our ADHD symptoms.

- In the future, what would you like to be able to say of yourself when you look back?

This cheat sheet is for when you're too sleepy or pressed for time to think things out in real-time and want to act on your values. Values and purpose statements can be written on a card kept at work, on your phone, or in your wallet.

5.4 ADHD BRAIN THINKING

The term "healing" refers to the process of "restoring wholeness." In order to recover and restore trust, we must be able to encapsulate the totality of who we are in a single image that includes a broad set of qualities. This means we need to stop focusing exclusively on our problems or our strengths.

Step 1: Get off the self-help bandwagon.
Many women with ADHD are extremely critical of themselves, in part because they have been raised on a steady diet of shame. Because they are embarrassed by their struggles, they believe that only by "fixing" themselves can they be able to live successfully.

Simply put, they believe that if they get organized and stop procrastinating, they will be satisfied (they take the class they have always put off and feel positive about themselves, for example). People with Attention Deficit Hyperactivity Disorder (ADHD) get so involved in managing their symptoms that they begin to believe they will never be happy if they don't treat their brains. This is, in fact, a complete reversal of logic.

ADHD is just a part of who you are, but it affects you because you can't avoid it. Everyone will ask, "Is it me, or is it my ADHD?" However, you and your ADHD are separate entities that are connected. When these factors are present, you get a complete individual. It is a positive step to recognize that our brains and bodies are intertwined.

Step 2: Adopt an attitude of "Yes, and…"

For me, healing is a holistic process that considers both an individual's strengths and needs to control symptoms. "I can pursue some of my aspirations and ambitions and improve my self-care" or "I am able to accomplish these things even though I still struggle" is what I have been advised and what I advise you to do. This shift away from unhealthy binary thinking has given me a new perspective on life by developing a more complete picture of myself. This is what I like to call the "yes, and" attitude.

Having moments where you wish your ADHD would just go away is perfectly normal. Only by reminding yourself that you are not "broken" can you find true healing. You'll begin to approach managing your problems with some self-compassion once you recognize that experiencing strengths and flaws at the same time is okay and completely normal.

Step 3: Recognize your personality traits.

You are well informed about the difficulties associated with ADHD. In fact, you've probably spent your entire life obsessing over them. To truly grasp who you are, you need to consider your values, strengths, and dreams. However, many people are unaware of or unable to these areas.

Step 4: Stay true to yourself and don't look to others for direction

We talk a lot about values and how important they are, but

we rarely act on them. Women with ADHD need to look inward and re-establish an internal compass to know what they want their life to look like.

Fix in your mind who you are and what matters to you when you feel like you're going in circles. Observing your internal compass will help you make smarter choices when you are lost or overwhelmed emotionally.

Your personal mission statement can be written as if you were running a business. If you think about it, you are in charge of your own destiny.

Step 5: Create a personal mission statement.
Craft your personal guide by honestly answering the following questions:

- What means the most to you?
- What do you believe in?
- What do you want to get done in your life?
- What do you consider your most important values?
- How do you want others to remember and see you?
- In the future, what do you wish you could say about yourself when you look back?

This cheat sheet is for when you are too lazy or have little time to think about things in real-time and want to act on your values. Values and purpose statements can be written on a card to keep on the countertop, phone, or in your wallet.

5.5 YOU'RE STUCK BECAUSE OF THESE 10 NEGATIVE THOUGHTS.

We are our own harshest critics. And because negative self-criticism can have significant health repercussions, it absolutely must be stopped.

We're all guilty of allowing a minor setback to turn into a cascade of self-critical and damaging thoughts. We are often our own harshest critics, resulting in significant health and self-esteem issues if we don't learn to control our negative ideas.

If you find yourself lingering or worrying about any of these ten typical corrosive thoughts, read on to learn how they can harm you in the long run—and how to rearrange your thoughts more positively and constructively.

'Instead of doing X, I should have done Y.'

'If I behave impeccably, I will be satisfied.'

'No one knows and understands what I'm saying.'

'I am stupid.'

'I am a failure.'

'I will start tomorrow.'

'I am constantly exploited.'

'My unhappiness is due to my ADHD.'

'I will never get what I want.

'This is impossible for me because of my ADHD.'

True, ADHD can make some situations more complicated. However, assuming that the difficulties it creates are insurmountable puts you at a perpetual disadvantage. Rather than surrender to a challenge made more difficult by your ADHD, embrace it. If you need assistance, seek it. If you need accommodations, make them known. With good treatment and support, you can accomplish great things on any scale.

5.6 15 MINDFUL HABITS YOUR BRAIN WANTS.

People with ADHD have a more robust emotional response than others. They become more engaging and exciting when they are happy and excited. Intense emotion, on the other hand, also has its drawbacks.

ADHD patients are impulsive. They get overwhelmed by their emotions and act without thinking about how their actions would affect others or themselves. You might become excited and forget the rest of your shopping list if you see something intriguing in the store.

This is where emotional self-control comes in: having the right feelings and emotions at the proper levels. People with ADHD suffer from both sides of the argument when it comes to getting things done.

They become fascinated by distractions and dissatisfied with the work they should be completing. They are unable to concentrate. They are unable to complete tasks. "Why am I always so emotional?" they may ask themselves.

Apply the brakes to a raging emotion.
A complete understanding of the problem is the first step to finding a good solution. Most of the emotional self-control tactics mentioned here are based on three fundamental ideas:

- Have strategies to control your emotions in the situations that trigger them.

- Manage your stress.

- Take responsibility for your reactions.

1. Take care of your stress. Everyone experiences stress and overwhelm from time to time. As much as possible, strive to reduce the number of demands you have on yourself at any given time.

2. Don't push yourself too hard. Everything seems to be exciting until we realize we have too much on our plate. You can reduce stress during the downturn by taking on less responsibility and gracefully dropping some duties when required—and with enough notice.

3. Get plenty of rest. When we get enough sleep, we are more optimistic and less reactive.

4. Exercise on a regular basis. Exercise is a great way to de-stress. It makes no difference how you exercise, as long as you do it regularly. Even a few push-ups or a brisk walk can help you clear your mind and put things in perspective.

5. Make time for yourself. Scheduling time for yourself to do something you enjoy is crucial. You'll burn yourself out if you don't recharge your batteries.

6. Address any co-occurring mood disorders. Anxiety and sadness are more common in adults with ADHD. These disorders, if left untreated, can devastate your emotional regulation, so it's best to seek expert help.

7. Stay away from emotionally charged situations. It is more challenging to control a hostile response than to prevent it from happening. This doesn't mean you can rule out every unpleasant or difficult scenario, but you should be aware that some aren't worth the risk.

8. Make your strategy. Prepare in advance on how to handle a scenario that you know will elicit strong emotions.

Consider how you would react to certain things another person might say or do, as well as the results you would like to achieve. Review the plan immediately before entering the scenario and keep it in mind throughout. If possible, bring written notes with you.

9. Take a break from what you are doing. If you have a choice between blowing up and leaving, it is preferable to go. Even 5 seconds might be enough to help you relax and collect your thoughts. If you're furious with someone you have a long-term connection with, tell them that taking a break will help you rearrange your thoughts and lead to a better conclusion for everyone.

10. Teach people not to criticize you. If you know, you're going to get emotional in specific situations—political debates, store sales—coach some of your friends and family to talk to you about the big picture or their point of view calmly. That way, you can reflect before you get caught up in a strong feeling.

11. No matter how intense your emotion is, it will pass. It could be a good feeling, like excitement about a possible purchase, or a terrible feeling, like a disastrous date. You'll still have the sense, but you'll be in a different mood.

12. Consider the other person's point of view. We react with the people we care about most. As much as we'd like to believe our feelings are justified, there are times when we react to someone for factors that have nothing to do with them. You will learn that things that have nothing to do with you should not be taken personally.

13. Distinguish between feeling and acting. Our emotions often influence our actions, but there is no apparent connection between the two. Observing how you feel and what makes you want to do without reacting is possible, although this is easier said than done. People can learn to do this through mindfulness training.

14. Share your emotional patterns with others. Explain to family, close friends, and possibly co-workers that you may be too passionate at first but that you will soon calm down and be able to have a meaningful conversation. This prevents them from overreacting to your response. You can also instruct them on how you want them to react when you have a wide range of emotions.

15. Explain what you really meant after you've calmed down. If things went wrong or you said something you didn't tell, explain your reasoning and what you meant to the person. Don't refute what the other person saw but let them know that your intentions were better than what you implied.

5.7 GETTING YOUR CONFIDENCE BACK

Self-confidence and self-esteem fluctuate over time in cyclical patterns. According to the study, self-esteem steadily improves with age, reaching a zenith around age 60. Gaining experience and professional accomplishments, achieving long-term goals, and having better financial security are just some reasons for this change. As people age, they have a greater sense of accomplishment in their lives.

Self-confidence and self-esteem do not increase with age for people with ADHD, and as they approach retirement, they actually decrease. This group of people is frustrated and challenged, and as a result, they believe they are disappointed in multiple ways. Many people have lost hope after making numerous unsuccessful attempts to modify their behavior. Because their financial planning has been haphazard at best and their long-term budgeting has not been carefully done, they may feel overwhelmed about their financial future as well.

Fortunately, even people with ADHD can rebuild their self-esteem and confidence as they age. For treating ADHD, you must eliminate the dark thinking that damages one's perspective of oneself; remember that this is critical to succeed in treatment.

Practical reasons for regaining confidence

- Put an end to your self-destructive thoughts. Low self-esteem can lead to a decrease in confidence in your ability to grow and change. It is possible to overcome this feeling, but it will require effort and perseverance. Adults with ADHD who are "stuck" must recognize, analyze, and reject negative thoughts that lead back to low self-esteem in order to move forward.

- Although these negative signals present themselves as natural, they should never be accepted as such. Instead of taking these signals seriously, treat them as mental aberrations. Self-esteem is formed by appreciating and accepting a person for who they are. It will take time and effort to recharge one's self-esteem, but it is a battle worth fighting.

- ADHD, mainly if not managed effectively, can lead to irritation and negative thoughts about oneself. Cumulative frustrations, criticism, perceived and actual failures, self-condemnation, and shame destroy self-esteem. Low self-esteem can also promote other significant problems such as anxiety, substance abuse, and other mental disorders.

5.8 REBUILDING YOUR SELF-ESTEEM AFTER ADHD DIAGNOSIS

It's difficult to undo and unlearn a lifetime's worth of shame and low self-esteem when you're diagnosed with ADHD in your 40s or 50s. If you've been in a state of shock since receiving your diagnosis, now is the time to begin regaining your strength. Give yourself a new name. The truth is, you're not damaged and never were. It's time to figure out what processes work best for you to accomplish the mission you were given. Here are six ways to regain your self-esteem after being diagnosed with ADHD. This is in your hands!

- **Get involved in something you enjoy doing.**

Dopamine levels are increased when a tasty result is experienced.

- **Be kind to yourself.**

Recognize your greatness and tell yourself that you are. You have to consistently reaffirm your self-worth when faced with a challenging task.

- **Embrace who you are right now.**

Now, don't be content with where you are now, but rather, accept it and move forward. It is what it is, and things will improve in time. You'll make progress in some areas and have setbacks in others, but as long as you don't give up, everything will be fine.

- **Become a member of a web forum dedicated to praising achievements.**

You don't want to be a part of an online community where everyone is always moaning about the difficulties of having ADHD. Outside noise is something you need to eliminate from your life. On the other hand, an online group where people can be encouraged through difficulties and celebrated for their achievements is critical.

- **Turn off any external noise sources.**

It's essential that you maintain a laser-like focus at all times. Put yourself in the situation. Determine if you've been daydreaming or if you've been sucked into social media or television. Make the most of your time.

5.9 REJECTION SENSITIVE DYSPHORIA AND ADHD

The response to rejection or criticism can cause RSD, which is an overwhelming emotional reaction. In fact, it is a condition that can lead to depression and low self-esteem.

A person suffering from RSD may feel rejected by an innocent comment or view a small argument as extremely serious.

It is possible that people internalize this intense emotional feeling, leading to depression and a desire to withdraw from the circumstance. Alternatively, people may express their feelings by becoming enraged or irrational out of the blue.

RSD can be a severe condition for both the sufferer and those around them, and it can wreak havoc on personal relationships. When someone reacts angrily or impulsively to a perceived offense, it can also lead to a brutal conflict.

The link between ADHD and RSD

ADHD is associated with a high threshold for rejection. There are neurological and genetic components that demonstrate this. RSD is not caused by trauma in early childhood, but it can worsen other conditions, including anxiety and depression. People find comfort in knowing that their symptoms have a name. Having an understanding of what it is and knowing that almost all people with ADHD have sensitivity to rejection makes a significant difference. They are happy to receive the diagnosis because it makes it clear that they are not to blame or harmed in any way.

Psychotherapy does not benefit people with RSD because of the abrupt and complete overpowering of the mind and senses by emotions that occur during sessions. Recovery from an episode of RSD is slow for those who suffer from it.

RSD can resemble a full-blown severe mood crisis, including suicidal ideation, when one internalizes this emotional reaction. The mood disorder is commonly mistaken as the rapid swing from feeling good to terribly unhappy due to RSD.

Sometimes, clinicians don't realize that these symptoms stem from the abrupt mood changes related to ADHD's sensitivity to rejection; in fact, RSD is a common symptom of ADHD, especially in women.

The externalization of this emotional response appears as a powerful and rapid rage against the situation or person that caused the pain.

RSD may cause adults with ADHD to overestimate their chances of being rejected, even when it is unlikely. This can cause individuals to become overly cautious when confronted with it, making some mistakes due to social anxiety. The hallmark of social phobia is the fear of embarrassing oneself or humiliating oneself in front of others by being evaluated harshly by the outside world.

It is difficult to tell if someone is overly sensitive to rejection or not. It is common for people to be at a loss for words when describing their suffering. It is described as intense, horrible, terrible, and overwhelming by those who have experienced it. The loss of love, approval, or respect always serves as a catalyst.

There are two basic approaches for people with ADHD to deal with this huge emotional elephant, and they do not overlap.

1. They develop a desire to please others. They do a background check on everyone they meet to see what they admire and appreciate. After that, they expose their falsified selves to others. Often, this goal takes over their life to the point that they lose sight of what they really want from them. To ensure that others are not dissatisfied, they will not have time for themselves.

2. They give up trying. Trying something new becomes too difficult or risky if there is even a remote chance of failing or falling short in the eyes of others. A high percentage of smart, talented people avoid tasks that cause them anxiety because they don't want to risk losing the esteem others place in them (both professionally and socially).

RSD pain may demotivate some people to develop workarounds and aspire to greater heights. They put endless effort into being the best at everything they do. Sometimes they feel a strong desire to be beyond reproach. But at what cost?

Self-Test "Do you have RSD"?
Even though persons with ADHD find it difficult to articulate rejection sensitivity dysphoria, everyone experiencing it can attest to how bad they feel. Dysphoria literally means "unbearable" in Greek. In many cases, persons with RSD try to hide their extreme emotional reactions from others because they are embarrassed by their openness. If you have RSD, you may have a deep and pervasive sense of failure, as if you have not met personal or external standards.

Is it possible that you have RSD, and that's the reason why you're so emotional? Use this self-test to see if you have symptoms of ADHD, and then meet with an experienced specialist to go over treatment options.

Fear of criticism and rejection prevents you from meeting new people or attempting new things.

Very Often

Often

Never

Rarely

Do you think you'll be able to cope with your feelings in any situation?

Very Often

Often

Never

Rarely

Do you worry about getting terminated every time your employer calls you into her office because you expect the worst?

Very Often

Often

Never

Rarely

Do you avoid close friendships or sexual connections because you're afraid people won't like you if they know "the real you"?

Very Often

Often

Never

Rarely

Do you worry about the possibility of depression that may result from your ADHD?

Very Often

Often

Never

Rarely

Are you ashamed of your "lack of control" over your emotions?

Very Often

Often

Never

Rarely

Do you ever have bodily reactions to your emotions, like if you've been physically "wounded?"

Very Often

Often

Never

Rarely

Do you devote more time to a job than is necessary, or do you become perfectionistic to doing that your work is error-free (and above reproach)?

Very Often

Often

Never

Rarely

Because of your intense emotional reactions, have you been labeled as "overly sensitive" or a "head case"?

Very Often

Often

Never

Rarely

Do you turn down opportunities or postpone starting tasks because you're frightened of failing?

Very Often

Often

Never

Rarely

Do you think of yourself as a "people pleaser," going out of your way to please others?

Very Often

Often

Never

Rarely

Do you become nervous in social environments because you believe no one likes you?

Very Often

Often

Never

Rarely

Are you the hardest critic of yourself?

Very Often

Often

Never

Rarely

Do you have abrupt, acute feelings of great melancholy when you believe you have been criticized and rejected?

Very Often

Often

Never

Rarely

Do you suffer sudden, strong fits of rage when your emotions are hurt?

Very Often

Often

Never

Rarely

5.10 HOW TO LIVE MORE AUTHENTICALLY WITH ADHD?

These five tactics can help you handle unpleasant symptoms and re-empower yourself instead of making excuses or striving for unrealistic perfection:

1. The 5x5 rule. Do you often find yourself endlessly criticizing yourself when you make a mistake? Consider using the "5x5 rule" if this is the case: Your friend's carpet is stained because you spilled red wine on it. So what? In five years, this will be entirely forgotten by your memory, so don't waste your time and attention ruminating on it. Give yourself 5 minutes to feel guilt, anger, or shame, and then try to let it go.

Of course, it's not always feasible to let go of anger. Instead of thinking of the 5x5 system, as a rule, you should adhere to it at all costs, consider it a goal.

2. Keep an ear out for the voice in your head and correct it when it's not friendly. Self-deprecating thoughts can become so commonplace for women with ADHD that we don't even notice them anymore. Even if we don't consciously hear these thoughts, they nonetheless have an impact on our lives. Whenever you can, bring these thoughts to light and contradict them.

3. When you make a mistake in the future, pay attention to your thoughts. If you find yourself thinking, "I'm just stupid" or "I can't do anything right," clear your head of these thoughts and move on. Regardless of the outcome, remember that you did the best you could under the situation. Remind yourself. What can you learn from this experience to avoid making the same mistakes again? After that, attempt to get rid of the bad thoughts in your head. Recognizing negative thoughts—and then respectfully showing them the exit—will help you build self-awareness and recover some of your lost power.

Make a new interpretation of your symptoms. Many women find that studying ADHD gives them a sense of control over their symptoms; notwithstanding, reading about attention deficiency's adverse consequences and results can be exhausting. If ADHD horrific stories and sobering statistics have you down, consider seeing your most troubling symptoms in a new light. Impulsive? That's a good thing since it implies you're a free spirit. Are you easily swayed? Well, you're able to pick up on details that others overlook because they're too busy working; this does not indicate that you will no longer be affected by these symptoms or not have difficulties resulting from them. However, focusing on the positive aspects of your ADHD rather than the negative ones will help you uncover your strengths, your peculiarities, and the methods and strategies that are most effective for you.

4. Strive to live a life that is true to yourself. Women with attention deficit hyperactivity disorder (ADHD) often conceal their symptoms by using masks. When we're screaming on the inside, we put on a happy front and act like everything is alright. It's tiring to keep our true selves hidden, yet we frequently don't have a choice.

5. Rekindle your passions and aspirations. In your childhood, what did you aspire to be? What about when you were an adolescent or a young adult full of hope? As we get older, we usually lose sight of our dreams, but they're still an essential component of us, and they can assist us in dealing with ADHD and promote the best version of ourselves.

Find some of the long-forgotten dreams of your past and start making efforts toward realizing them. This does not imply quitting your day job to pursue a career as a ballerina! Taking out a library book might be as simple as discovering that you're still passionate about marine biology after all. It may imply joining a recreational sports team or booking a trip to a fascinating new destination for a fun getaway.

The essential thing in life is creating new possibilities and reaching your maximum potential.

To live truthfully, without guises or excuses, is your new journey. Some women will benefit from therapy or the guidance of a life coach; others will find that knowing themselves, flaws and virtues, makes them feel more empowered. You don't have to be "fixed" no matter what path you choose. We are unique and extraordinary women, and we will never be defined by either our ADHD or our past failures! Believe in the process, believe in yourself, and believe in the strength that has always been within you.

CHAPTER 6: EXERCISE AND HEALTHY EATING

ADHD can make it harder to pay attention, regulate one's emotions, and complete the various tasks of your day. Therapy and medication treatments can be used to help you become structured and stay focused.

Exercise is a type of ADHD treatment that does not require medication or the 'assignment to a therapist; regular physical activity increases thinking skills, so it can also help with symptoms. In addition, it can help maintain a healthy brain.

When you exercise, your brain produces neurotransmitters, such as dopamine, that help concentrate and clarify thought. Women with ADHD often have lower levels of dopamine in their brains than average.

Stimulant medications are often used to treat adult ADHD by increasing the availability of dopamine in the brain. So, it makes sense that exercise may have some of the same impacts as stimulant medications.

Adult women with ADHD may benefit from the following fitness benefits:

- Increase self-control and decrease obsessive behavior.
- Help relieve tension and anxiety.
- Increase working memory.
- Increase the amounts of neurotrophic factors generated by the brain. These proteins play a role in memory and learning. It is scarce in individuals with ADHD.
- Strengthen executive function, which is the set of skills needed to plan, organize and remember details.

6.1 ADHD-FRIENDLY SPORTS FOR WOMEN

Swimming
Women with ADHD can help themselves with the structure and guidance, which a swim team can provide. Women swimmers benefit from critical one-on-one time with instructors while participating in team activities. You can focus on personal development—specifically, encouraging personal swim times—without having to compete against others. Michael Phelps, an Olympian, says swimming helped him manage his ADHD symptoms early on by keeping him focused and disciplined.

Tennis
Tennis is a great sport for women who flourish as they struggle against themselves to gain new skills. Tennis needs a coordinated effort and communication when playing doubles. Yet, its energetic, fast pace keeps women focused for an extended period of time—a bonus for many women with ADHD. Also, hitting tennis balls could be a great outlet for your anger or frustration after a difficult day at work.

Martial Arts

Discipline, self-control, and respect are just a few of the traits that martial arts instructors teach. Through step-by-step training, women have learned each new martial arts combo—leaving little room for distraction. An interesting factor of martial arts is the use of traditions, such as kneeling to the master, which can help women with ADHD accept, develop and use the routine in other parts of their lives.

Yoga

Yoga, for example, has been shown in studies to help women with ADD and ADHD improve their concentration. Yoga equipment and exercises are identical to those used in therapy. They can help manage sensory processing disorder by strengthening the core, developing a sense of balance, and increasing muscle awareness.

Horseback Riding

Horses have the ability to mimic the emotions and attitudes of their handlers, which is used in equine-assisted psychotherapy (EAP). When a woman with ADD connects with the horse, she will do so by watching and responding to the animal's behaviors rather than repeating her own.

Running

Cross-country running requires minimal time and no cost (except buying a good pair of running shoes). Running encourages discipline and pace, and the woman with ADHD will also benefit from the company of a few friends who can train with her.

6.2 MOTIVATIONAL TIPS TO STAY ON TRACK

Are you eager to start your new fitness regimen? Changing your exercise habits will be much easier once you start noticing the benefits.
Here are six of my favorite concepts to stay on track.

1. Take responsibility for your actions.
Allow yourself to exercise if you've made a promise to yourself to do so. You still have time, even if it's 10:30 pm. If going outside or to the gym isn't an option, try doing push-ups or jumping jacks on the spot instead. You want to end the day by declaring, "I kept my promises!

2. Make working out a "win-win" situation.
Many individuals with ADHD set themselves up for failure by having unreasonably high expectations for themselves when they work out. People who commit to working out for 40 minutes but only manage to do 20 may be disappointed and decide to give up on their next workout.

Rather, consider this alternative: Start by determining how much activity you consider acceptable—for example, 15 minutes twice a week at the gym. Set a reasonable time limit for your workouts, such as 30 minutes a day, five days a week. There's a strong chance you'll reach your minimum goal with ease, and even better, you'll probably exceed it. Trying to reach your goals gives you a sense of accomplishment and motivates you to keep working out. Be sure to consistently increase your minimum and maximum goals.

3. Keep a log of your workouts.
Mark the days you work out with an "X" on your calendar. You don't have to measure time, number of reps, number of times you do a specific exercise or your heart rate, or anything else. Review your results once a month to measure your development.

4. Schedule additional workouts as a "safety net."
Most people with ADHD despise structure, particularly when it comes to doing exercises and performing other "tasks." Add some leeway to your structure by planning not one but several workouts over the course of a single day. You can, for example, schedule your weekend workout for Saturday at 11 am, 2 pm, and 4 pm, and Sunday at 11:30 am, 3:30 pm, and 6 pm. There are a total of six chances to get it right. There's a good chance you'll stick with one of these ideas.

5. Write down your motivation.
Many people with ADD/ADHD start an exercise routine with great enthusiasm but quickly lose motivation. If this describes your situation, send a note of encouragement. Ask a friend to "deliver it" to you when your motivation wanes during the first few weeks of an exercise regimen.

6. Keep your "inner saboteur" at bay.
If a voice inside your head keeps urging, "Why not skip today's workout and do it tomorrow instead?" it will be difficult to create regular exercise routines. There is almost always a voice in the person's head when they have ADHD. It's not worth paying attention to. Tell it to go away and tell it again to never come back.

6.3 HEALTHY EATING FOR ADHD BRAINS

Many women with ADHD are in constant conflict with healthy eating habits. Why? Every day, we make dozens of decisions about food and eating that require strong executive functions; our ADHD minds must anticipate, organize, coordinate, and execute smart food choices to maintain a healthy, nutritious diet. When we fail, we feel demoralized and blame our ADHD symptoms.

1. Eat Consciously and Mindfully

Adults with ADHD don't pay attention to the details of what they're eating. They consume fewer healthful items and consume more junk food than they realize. Even if they dislike it, they eat more of it and in larger portions. Take a good, hard look at your eating patterns before making any adjustments. This is how it works:

- Keep track of everything you consume in a week. Whether you write down on a notebook, make a note on your smartphone, or even make a photo of your meal before eating, make sure you remember what you're eating. Consider what you ate and check to see if it matches a healthy food intake before looking at your messages or images at the end of the day or week. You're going to be shocked!

- Eat while sitting at a table. Although it may seem obvious, individuals with ADHD are more likely to consume food while engaged in other activities, sometimes sitting on the couch or even standing. To prevent your brain from labeling every house's area as a possible "dining room," make sure you eat at a real dining table.

- Plan when you'll eat. Focus on hunger cues instead of boredom when trying to eat. This is an example of a daily eating schedule:

Breakfast at 7 a.m.

Snack at 10 a.m.

Lunch at 12 p.m.

Snack at 4 p.m.

Dinner at 7 p.m.

- Keep an eye on your serving sizes. The volume-craving brain of an ADHS sufferer. Using smaller bowls and plates is one way to get around this. Irrespective of the size of the bowl, eating a whole serving of something will leave you feeling content.

2. Stop Eating on the Spot

ADHD is characterized by a high level of impulsivity, which manifests itself in our eating patterns. Having eaten to the point of discomfort and regret is common after bingeing on excessive food. Adolescents and adults with ADHD often eat more quickly, which can contribute to overeating because your stomach doesn't have enough time to inform your brain that you are satisfied. To prevent binge eating, use the following methods:

- Before you eat a meal, take 3 to 5 deep breaths.
- Drink some water first thing in the morning before anything else. When you're eating, drinking a glass of water may help you feel full faster.
- To become a more attentive eater, even 20 seconds of grounding each day can make a difference.
- After each bite, put your spoon or fork down. Wait to use the utensil or eat more until you've finished the current portion.
- Put some space between yourself and the serving basin after scooping your piece. If you don't have to stand up to obtain another serving, you're more likely to desire a

third. Fast access means you'll have less time to question whether or not you're actually still hungry when you get there.

- Make it difficult for people to get their hands on munchies. Stack the Oreos on top of one another in the pantry cabinet. When something is hidden, it is easier to forget about it. When you see certain meals that trigger your appetite, you may "realize" that you are no longer satisfied.

3. Do not eat when you are agitated or angry.
When things go tough, many people turn to a pint of ice cream for comfort. Women with ADHD, who have trouble controlling their emotions, are particularly prone to this.

- Take 5 minutes whenever you feel agitated or furious to slow down and breathe deeply to re-center yourself. Avoid overeating and instead turn to relaxing activities such as yoga or massage to feel better. A different sensory input may be preferable to food when it comes to providing sensory relaxation.

- When you find yourself getting bored, pause and take notes. Plan out what you'll do when you're bored and write it down. Make a phone call to a close friend. Spend some time reading a book. Solve a riddle if you want to. A pastime is other than food preparation.

- You'll be more prone to mindless eating if you're experiencing bad feelings. You should take a break as soon as you notice them starting to come on. You'll be tempted to eat but resist the urge.

- Instead of resorting to impulsive eating, express your feelings creatively (via movement, singing, martial arts, etc.) or with the old standby of discussing to someone about your unpleasant day.

4. Follow the Directions on the Labels

Understandably, women with ADHD are perplexed by the amount of nutritional data accessible. Take the guesswork out with these simple ideas based on common sense.

- Include high-protein and high-fiber foods in your diet. If you have allergies or some dietary restrictions, a dietitian or your physician can advise you on what ailments to keep in your pantry (e.g., you're vegan).

- Always keep healthy essentials like fruit, vegetables, and lean protein in your house and on your shopping list. Often, we consume unhealthy foods simply because we don't have access to other options. The key to successful shopping is to use common sense. Foods such as:

Turkey, eggs, yogurt, fish, nuts, olive oil, vegetables, fruits, boneless chicken breast.

- Don't take in calories by drinking them. Sodas are little more than sugar in a liquid form. In addition, even though diet soda claims to have no sugar, it actually contains a lot of artificial sweeteners, which might lead to obesity. Replace soda with flavored seltzer water a few times per week. Due to their high caloric content and ability to reduce inhibitions, alcoholic beverages might lead to impulsive behavior. Keep in mind, too, that juicing your fruits isn't the same as consuming them in terms of nutrition as you may think. This increases sugar levels because juicing them removes much of the fiber.

- Check the ingredients' names on the package. We frequently misjudge a food's caloric or fat content. See what is on the label to see if it is safe to consume it. Look out for the nutritional information on your takeout order before ordering, so you know exactly how much fat, sugar, and sodium are in it. Not eating certain foods can have an even greater influence on our health.

5. Be Conscious of the Bigger Picture

Adults with ADHD mean well, but their actions don't always match their words. More than just good intentions are required if we are to make any progress. We need a strategy, as well as the development of good behaviors that extend beyond food.

- Get plenty of rest. Sleep deprivation amplifies the symptoms of ADHD and contributes to excessive weight gain. When a person does not have enough sleep, their body's metabolism slows, and fat is stored. You feel that you are not relaxing because there is a greater need (food) at stake.

- Plan your weekly meals ahead by setting up an hour each week (ideally on the weekend). Look in your cupboard and refrigerator to see if you have everything you need. Make a list of all the things you'll need and go shopping for them. Next week, when you've had a long day at work, this preparation will make decision-making easier. Turn on your favorite tunes, brew yourself a cup of coffee, and get to work. Spending an hour doing this every week can save you time and energy.

- Do some physical activity! Our metabolism, cognitive clarity, mood, and ADHD symptoms will improve when we regularly do physical activity.

- Foodies don't have to abandon their passion for culinary exploration just because they want to eat healthfully and mindfully. It's not a mystery that people with ADHD have a strong attachment to food. It's a party for the eyes, ears, and nose. Eating healthy will increase, not detract from, our enjoyment of food. We'll appreciate flavors more and feel more emotionally connected to textures and scents. Later, we can develop a stronger relationship with it. In addition, maintaining a healthy weight extends the amount of time you may spend savoring delectable meals.

- It took the Romans several years to build the city of Rome. Don't be too unforgiving with yourself if you occasionally give in to mindless eating. It is something that everyone does. And with perseverance, you will learn to avoid it. Think about what caused you to consume the wrong things instead of feeling defeated.

6.4 DIET TO HELPS YOU STAY FOCUSED

Is it possible that what you eat can help you pay attention, concentrate, or control your hyperactivity? There isn't enough scientific evidence to affirm that a poor diet or nutritional deficiencies contribute to ADHD. However, some research suggests that certain foods may influence symptoms in a subset of people.

Children and adults with ADHD who are malnourished are more easily impulsive, distracted, and restless. Instead of worsening those symptoms, eating the appropriate meals at the appropriate time will become your new good habit.

Nutrition That Boosts Your ADHD Brain
ADHD medications benefit many adults and children, although they do not work for everyone. Supplements and food can aid ADHD brains that are short on (and urgently seeking) dopamine if the medication cannot be used.

ADHD cannot be cured with only medication, and medication should never be the primary treatment used to address the condition. Proper nutrition is essential for the ADHD brain's proper functioning.

Accordingly, in this chapter, you will find natural remedies for ADHD that you should include in your treatment plan for increased focus, attention, and motivation, including meal suggestions, ADHD pills, and herbs.

The best thing for your safety is to consult with your doctor before making any changes to your current treatment regimen.

ADHD-Controlling Proteins

In order to generate neurotransmitters—the chemicals discharged by brain cells to interact with one other—the body uses protein-rich foods like nuts, lean beef, poultry, pork, fish, beans, and eggs. Protein helps stabilize blood sugar levels, which reduces hyperactivity. When you consume protein, your body produces brain-awakening neurotransmitters, so have a protein-rich breakfast first thing in the morning.

ADHD Balanced Meals

The following is how you should split your lunch and supper plates: Half of the plate should consist of fruits and vegetables, one-fourth of the plate should have protein, and the final one-fourth of the plate should contain carbohydrates, preferably one high in fiber—brown rice, whole wheat grain bread, and pasta.

This mix of foods will reduce behavioral fluctuations due to hunger or vitamin deficiency. Fiber helps persons with attention deficit disorder (ADD) avoid blood sugar swings that can exacerbate symptoms of inattention.

6.5 NATURAL SUPPLEMENTS AND VITAMINS TO TREAT ADHD

Daily meals for many individuals are deficient in important vitamins and minerals, which can help people focus and stay occupied. Dopamine-boosting supplements (fish oil, vitamin D, etc.) can typically make up for nutritional deficiencies.

While medication can help many children and adults with ADHD, it does not eradicate all symptoms. Natural therapies, such as exercise, vitamins, and herbs, might enhance every therapy strategy.

Nutritionists that specialize in ADHD recommend consuming complex carbs, vegetables, fruits, and lean protein. Even yet, our systems may require additional nutrients that are best given through supplements.

These minerals and vitamins are the most frequently prescribed for the treatment of ADHD symptoms.

- **Melatonin**

Melatonin is the natural hormone in our bodies that aids us with sleep. This supplement may assist in calming racing minds that do not easily go asleep.

- **Omega-3s**

Fatty acids present in cold-water fish such as sardines and salmon may aid in the improvement of:

- Cognitive skills
- Behavior
- Focus

According to studies, ADHD-optimized doses of Omega-3s are around 40% as efficient as stimulant medication.

- **B Vitamins for Individuals with ADHD**
  - According to studies, supplementing children with

insufficient B vitamins increased mental acuity and decreased hostility and antisocial behavior. Vitamin B-6 appears to enhance dopamine levels in the brain, which promotes alertness.

- To acquire: Pharmacy chains sell B vitamin formulations at a reasonable price. Various research on vitamin B and attention deficit hyperactivity disorder (ADHD) have been done on a Swiss product called Bio-Strath.

- **Iron, Zinc, and Magnesium for ADHD**

- Zinc aids in the production of dopamine and enhances the effects of methylphenidate. Low concentrations of this mineral are associated with inattention. These substances may help to reduce impulsivity and hyperactivity.

- Iron is crucial for the synthesis of dopamine. Ferritin levels (a marker of iron reserves) were low in 84% of ADHD women compared to 16% of the control group in one small study. Iron deficiency is associated with cognitive impairment and severe ADHD.

- Adequate magnesium levels have a relaxing effect on the brain. While increasing mineral levels through food is the safest route, a multivitamin supplement will guarantee that you receive the daily reference value for all three.

- Ginseng and Ginkgo for ADHD

- Many children and adults benefit moderately from the mineral-vitamin approach. Those with more severe ADHD may require more medication—specifically, botanicals.

- These herbs are stimulants of the mind. They operate similarly to stimulants but without adverse side effects. Children and adults who take ginseng and ginkgo score higher on ADHD rating measures and exhibit reduced impulsivity and distraction. Asian ginseng may cause hyperactivity in younger children. If this occurs, switch your youngster to American ginseng.

- **Pycnogenol for Attention**
- According to standardized tests and teacher and parent ratings, Pycnogenol, an extract derived from French maritime pine bark, was reported to reduce hyperactivity and increase concentration, attention, and visual-motor synchronization in students after a month.
- Pycnogenol is also high in polyphenols, which act as antioxidants, protecting brain cells from damage caused by free radicals.
- **Multimineral/Multivitamins for ADHD**
- If you're a picky eater or frequently order takeout food, you'll be missing out on the necessary daily intake of vitamins and minerals. Daily multimineral/multivitamin supplementation will ensure you do, no matter how picky you are.
- **Rhodiola Rosea for ADHD**
- This herb, derived from the same-named plant which grows in the Arctic, has been shown to increase attention, alertness, and accuracy. It may be overly stimulating for small children, but it is occasionally suitable for youngsters aged eight to twelve. Brown notes that it is especially beneficial for students in high school, junior high, and college who are required to write lengthy essays and spend several hours reading.
- **Vitamin C**
- Vitamin C plays a critical role in regulating the neurotransmitter dopamine at brain synapses. Vitamin C should not be taken within an hour after taking ADHD medication.

CHAPTER 7: SLEEP & MORNINGS

Many children and adults with ADHD have difficulty falling asleep and staying asleep. Sleep can easily be disrupted by physical and mental restlessness, which can have a negative effect on an individual's ADHD therapy.

These ADHD-friendly rituals will help you calm your rushing mind and help you fall asleep more easily:

Caffeine

Don't: Consume anything caffeinated less than 4 hours before night (including caffeinated tea, coffee, and chocolate). Caffeine, like liquor, is a stimulant and a diuretic, which may urge you to wake up to need the restroom.

Do: Consume chamomile tea. Chamomile has a slight sedative effect, which is amplified by the calming effect of a warm beverage.

Medications & Conditions

Don't: Take some drugs before going to bed. Numerous OTC pain drugs contain a significant amount of caffeine—more than a cup of coffee! Certain asthma drugs, migraine, cold treatments, and antidepressants all can cause insomnia.

Do: Assess and/or treat restless legs syndrome (RLS). The name of this widespread sleep condition refers to the "creepy, crawly" feeling in the legs of sufferers, which creates a want to move and makes falling asleep difficult.

Eating & Showering

Don't: Consume a substantial meal. A meal takes approximately four hours to digest, which can keep you up, so eat early.

Do: Consume little snacks. When you go for a long period of time without eating, your body sends signals to boost blood sugar levels.

Do: An hour before bed, take a hot bath or shower. This will relax and calm your muscles and signal to your body that it is time to sleep.

Drinks

Don't: Consume alcoholic beverages. Alcohol consumption can impair your ability to sleep and may end in frequent waking. Alcohol is a stimulant and will also cause multiple nighttime bathroom visits.

Do: Consume warm milk. Milk includes tryptophan, the same organic sedative found in turkey, and it may be enough to calm even the most hyperactive ADHD mind.

7.1 9 SOLUTIONS TO SLEEP DEPRIVATION FOR INDIVIDUALS WITH ADHD

ADHD and sleep deprivation frequently interact. How? Our racing brains, impulsive behavior, and ineffective time management keep us awake far too late. Then, as a result of exhaustion, our symptoms become worse, and the cycle repeats. Here's how to regain control of your sleep.

1. Increase Hours
While 8 hours of sleep is ideal, even dropping from 5 to 5 and a half hours creates a noticeable change in how you feel. A five-hour night may not seem so horrible if you've already enjoyed several seven-hour nights, as the advantages of sleep can be progressive. Therefore, give yourself recognition for your development. And irrespective of how well you slept last night, make today one remember.

2. Consistent Sleep
Sleeping late on Sat and Sun isn't enough to make you feel better if you are sleep-deprived. Indeed, yo-yo-ing between short periods of sleep through the week and extended sleep on weekends disrupts your sleep/wake cycle, leaving your body unsure of whether to be alert or when to change gear

into sleep mode. It may take another week or three of regular sleep for your system to adjust its clock and for you to develop an awareness of what it feels like to be "rested." And, in comparison, how worse you felt before getting consistent sleep.

3. Consider Tomorrow

Choosing to stay up very late is about savoring the moment while incurring a cost in the future. This is alluring, even more so for people with ADHD. To help you resist this temptation:

1. Consider what tomorrow would be like if you remained up too late.

2. Consider how difficult it is to pull oneself out of bed, how frustrating it is to hurry to work, and how long a day feels when you are exhausted and sleepy.

3. Consider how much better your day will be if you get a decent night's sleep.

4. Establish a Sleep Schedule

Many of my sleep-deprived clients do not have a consistent bedtime. It may be 12 a.m. or 2 a.m. This ambiguity may be deliberate, but it makes it difficult to manage time throughout the night, as there is no deadline against which to order time. As a result, establish a bedtime and treat it as you would a job deadline. Calculate time backward from that point to organize your evening and make a concerted effort to adhere to it.

5. Eliminate Naps

While naps can refuel you for the remainder of the day, they can also contribute to the problem. If you take a 15-minute power nap in the afternoon, you are not getting sufficient sleep at night. Long naps (1 to 2 hours) are a sure sign that you are not receiving enough sleep and also interrupt your wake/sleep/ cycle, making it hard to fall asleep at a decent time. This sets you up for another lengthy slumber the next day. Break the cycle by struggling along without taking a nap and going to bed on time – tonight will be miserable, but tomorrow will be great.

6. Make a List of the Barriers You Face

Make a list of the reasons why you're unable to fall asleep at a reasonable time. It's important to ask yourself: Is it mainly about "immediate causes," like staying up late on Facebook? Do you think it's more about "far causes," such as arriving late and needing to work late in order to complete the project? First, what happens when the first dominoes fall? Do you know the triggers that can change the course of the day or night? These are the common questions on where you can have the greatest impact.

7. Reexamine Your Medications

Extended-release stimulants can help you get through the day at work, but how long will they last into the evening? Talk to your doctor about adding a late-afternoon dose if your day is functioning well, but you're having trouble sleeping at night. Taking too much medicine might cause sleep problems for some people, but untreated ADHD makes it more difficult to keep track of the daily schedule and get to bed on time. Get to know how things work best for you.

8. Let Go of the Lie You're Telling Yourself

We tell ourselves minor lies in order to be able to do things we know we shouldn't be able to do. Even if you may think you don't need as much sleep as you think you do, it's important to note that you can always compensate for it on the weekends. Also, you may overestimate how long a task will take and then engage in it on a whim, saying, "I'll just have a brief peek at social media platforms before I go to bed." If we're honest with ourselves, we'd admit that these small lies have some truth to them, but they're less true than we'd like them to be. So, remind yourself that these tiny lies are at best unduly positive and that you might inevitably be unhappy in the long run.

9. Ask yourself, "Why?"

Are you squandering your slumber in order to accomplish tasks that you would otherwise be unable to accomplish? Is staying awake a method to relax after a long day of work, or is it just a way to have some fun? These needs are legitimate, but are you making your life more difficult by depriving yourself of sleep? The trade-off may be possible at some other point in the future. Hold in there and try to come up with a solution that works for you. What has to be done in your life to make you happy and rested?

7.2 HAVE DIFFICULTY RISEN IN THE MORNING?

ADHD is characterized by arousal and motivation problems, as evidenced by scientific studies and clinical observations. In addition, research has shown that many individuals with ADHD have difficulties sleeping at the usual time as the rest of people because their circadian rhythms are out of whack.

No matter what time they go to bed, women with ADHD have difficulty falling asleep before 12 p.m., and their minds remain in a half-wakeful state until they have to leave the bed.

It's easy to see that just getting out of bed is a difficult task, especially when you consider that they may be naturally disorganized, suffer from slow processing, have transition issues, or have a poor sense of time. This is not to argue that they should absolve themselves of their obligations but rather point out that they may need additional help and skills to succeed.

Tips That Help

Maintaining a good night's sleep is critical to a person's overall health, mental well-being, and productivity. For most women, 8 to 9 hours of undisturbed sleep is considered "plenty."

- Make sure you're doing your best to go to sleep at a "decent" hour by reviewing your nightly routine and doing everything you can to make the mornings less stressful. Packing your bag, checking the weather forecast, and deciding what to wear are just a few of the tasks that can be done the night before to ensure everything that needs to be brought along is in a consistent location.

- Make use of a variety of alarm clocks. Some people can be woken up by music, while others need a loud noise to wake up. You can choose from a lot of unique and interesting solutions.

- Adopt a two-alarm system if you use stimulant medication. If medication needs to be administered, the first alarm could go off a half-hour to an hour before the scheduled wake-up time. In this way, women will be able to get out of bed more easily since the medication has had time to work its magic.

- Lack of motivation can be a big problem for some women with ADHD. Probably they may not be able to focus on starting their day because they are thinking about how deeply they would like to sleep. It is important to visualize how it feels to be successful. You might be motivated by a picture of you achieving your goal or anything that reminds you of what you really want to be and achieve

CHAPTER 8: ANXIETY AND STRESS

8.1 ANXIETY AND ADHD: CONNECTIONS SYMPTOMS AND COPING MECHANISMS

Anxiety and attention deficit hyperactivity disorder (ADHD) are intimately linked. Since the ADHD experience creates a life filled with tension and concern, anxiety illness is the most common comorbidity for those with ADHD.

As a result, adults with ADHD, often known as ADD) are plagued by anxiety. Anxiety is crucial for people with ADHD because of the way the disorder affects their day-to-day lives.

That's why it's impossible to talk about ADHD without mentioning anxiety, whether it's a nagging worry about meeting deadlines or making tough back-to-school decisions or a full-blown anxiety condition. Anxiety is a common comorbid diagnosis for adult ADHD, and the connection between the two is clear.

The epidemic has exacerbated the link between ADHD and anxiety in today's society. This relationship is untenable to overlook because of a cloud of uncertainty that hangs over us.

Is Anxiety a Sign of ADHD?
Although anxiety is not a diagnostic requirement for ADHD, there is a substantial correlation between the two illnesses. More than half of women with attention deficit hyperactivity disorder suffer from anxiety.

Anxiety is the response to a perceived threat or risk in our minds and bodies. There are a variety of anxiety disorders, such as social anxiety disorder, panic attacks, post-traumatic stress disorder (PTSD), and more, all of which are characterized by continual feelings of dread and terror.

Is Anxiety Worsening Due to ADHD?
Anxiety symptoms are more intense in women with ADHD disorder than those without ADHD.

It's also possible that even those individuals with ADHD who don't fulfill the criteria for anxiety may nevertheless suffer occasional and situational worry because of their ADHD, which can induce time blindness and poor working memory, among other anxiety-developing symptoms.

Anxiety is a common symptom in women with ADHD. It can be caused by a variety of factors, including delay or procrastination, the fear of being socially stigmatized, and the potential for social isolation.

Additional Anxiety-Inducing ADHD Symptoms
"Repeated Inconsistency"

Anxiety stems from a lack of certainty about the outcome of an event or a task. In order to appreciate the constant pressure of dealing with ADHD, it is essential to understand "continuous inconsistency." ADHD symptoms including inattention, overwhelm, and memory lapses can lead to "consistent inconsistency," a feeling of skepticism and uncertainty in oneself. For example, "consistent inconsistency" is knowing a work must be completed yet doubting one's own ability to complete it.

Performance Issues Caused by ADHD

Those with ADHD realize what they need to do, but struggle to do it, which causes them to worry. This is a high source of frustration for women with ADHD, especially as they get older. Some of the obstacles to accomplishment are listed below:

- How effective are you at self-regulation? I don't know whether or not I can resist the temptation to get distracted or lose my concentration.

- Optimism is based on a mistaken view of the world. It's been said, "I work better under pressure."

- "I have to be in the emotion/ the energy to do anything," says the person with front-end perfectionism. Adults with ADHD are considerably more prone to have distorted instinctive thoughts based on these implausible norms than the general population.

- Emotional dysregulation is a hallmark of ADHD, even though it isn't listed in the DSM-5. Being able to adjust and manage our emotional states in order to readily engage in an activity is a part of managing anxiety. Avoidance and procrastination can aggravate and be intensified by anxiety if discomfort is not appropriately handled.

8.2 HOW DO YOU HANDLE ANXIETY AND STRESS?

Medication and psychosocial therapy can be used to treat both ADHD and anxiety. Although it depends on the individual, the medication that targets one ailment often helps symptoms of the other. Despite this, doctors always begin with the most severe cases first.

When treating ADHD and anxiety at the same time, non-stimulant drugs are classified as second-line pharmacological therapy rather than stimulants. The most effective treatment for those with anxiety and ADHD is a mix of medication and treatment.

Healthy coping techniques might also help alleviate general anxiety.

Other Coping Mechanisms
- Movement and physical activity. When it comes to traditional workdays, we tend to underestimate how much "stealth" movement we give up. It's as simple as it may sound, but the movement is a good thing. This is especially true if you're confined to your home office. We can take a break from our daily routines and recharge our batteries when we move.

- Organize your free time. Creating a routine, especially a very visible one, can't be avoided. It could be a planner, an open digital calendar on a tablet, or an appointment book; it's essential to keep track of everything. We can use planners to see days, hours, and weeks into the future, which helps us prepare for what we want to accomplish. In any schedule, time must be set aside for breaks, including making room.

- Maintain a healthy lifestyle. Whether you have ADHD or not, many people are suffering from chronic stress and a general sense of overwhelming for no apparent reason. Stress can be reduced through better exercise, sleep, and diet.

- Make physical space arrangements. In order to encourage behavioral priming and habit formation, it is important to designate specific areas of the home for work, leisure, sleep, and other activities. Refreshing and preparing your workspaces for the next day can help reduce "sight pollution" and ease the passage from one day to the next.

- Keep taking your ADHD medication and see a therapist if necessary. As a result of medication, adults with ADHD are able to cope better and feel less anxious, making them more productive and less prone to depression. The same goes for online psychotherapy, which is becoming more and more commonplace.

- Decatastrophize. Even if a loved one has passed away, it is essential to maintain perspective and practice gratitude in order to get through this. It's a good idea to avoid thinking in terms of a rigid "should"—that is, if something doesn't go according to plan, it's not good. Having to accept some pessimistic thoughts for what they are—thoughts—can also help us "defuse."

- Defining tasks is the sixth step. Mark your calendar with tasks instead of vaguely defining activities. Checking email can take as little as 5 minutes or as long as 15 minutes to complete while evaluating a report for the job can be a 15-minute or 15-page task. Front-end perfectionism can be overcome by clearly laying out charges, which becomes a simple way of engaging in an assignment for which you are not 'in the mood.' After getting engaged, the pain subsides quickly.

- Don't expect too much from yourself. In this world, we can't expect the same results as others. That's a simple way to get yourself caught in a web of deception. It's time to shift our perspective and adopt a mindset of adequacy. Having a "good enough" mindset can help you break out of a rut and reduce your stress levels. It's probably not a good time to start a new career, but it could be an excellent time to tackle some long-overdue home improvement projects.

8.3 THE 9 STRESS-RELIEVING POINTS

Small steps can get you a long way. Start with one of these easy mindfulness methods today, and then try another one tomorrow. These small sums will quickly mount up.

Mindfulness is seen as a superpower for treating anxiety. Amid ADHD-induced chaos, seeking peace may be the only way to find solace.

You can cultivate mindfulness by attempting the following: Focus solely on your breathing by placing a palm on your tummy. Even if you get sidetracked, gradually bring your attention back to your breathing. Your focus and self-control will return once you've exercised your attention muscles and blocked out the stresses of daily life.

1. Observe The "Two Minute Rule."
Dentist appointments are a pain in the ass. Also, there's always the option of paying your monthly electricity payment.

It's often more emotionally draining and challenging to put off these small things than just go ahead and do them now. Follow this simple rule: if you can finish a task in under two minutes, do it right now. As a result, you'll be able to clear your mind and boost your self-esteem.

2. When It's Possible, Use Auto-Pay.

Many persons with ADHD have their electricity cut off because they have failed to pay their payments. By establishing an online banking account to electronically pay your monthly payments, you may avoid this embarrassment as well as the associated late fees.

You may choose to ask a tech-savvy buddy to assist you for a half-hour in order to overcome your apprehension. It's a low-risk, high-return investment that pays dividends for years to come.

3. Focus On One Task Each Day.

Get rid of your guilt and sense of helplessness over your mess! One square foot at a time is the most incredible method of getting things done.

Establish a daily goal of 15 minutes of productive work and stick to it. Clean out your kids' clothing, organize the pantry's cabinets, and pay all of your bills. To avoid getting overwhelmed, focus on one task at a time. Plus, it will take you the satisfaction of crossing things off your list.

4. Preparation Is Key.

It's a good idea to put an appointment in your calendar, but it's not sufficient on its own. Consider what must be done before work, such as locating your vehicle's registration or obtaining a specialist reference and adding them to your calendar.

Two things happen because you get more mentally prepared for the ahead job, and you develop a more logical strategy.

The next crucial step in this process is to check your planner or calendar numerous times a day.

5. Make Your To-Do List Less Exhausting.
Jotting down and then crossing off tasks on a to-do list may be a great sense of accomplishment. In some cases, simply making a big list of things you're responsible for is enough to cause you to feel anxious. You may not need to mention every single activity you have to complete, especially if some of them are unimportant or time-consuming. Only include the most important tasks and prioritize things so that each day can indeed be a step forward.

6. Allow Room For Growth.
It may be possible to get out of the house on time, but there is currently no way for me to do so. It's a potent reminder that you're on the road to development if you repeat this to yourself. Soon you will begin to think that the best version of you is being created right now and will only be revealed through perseverance and diligence.

7. Think Positively.
Even on the days when you think of yourself as a total scumbag, write down three things you're proud of about yourself. Unless you acknowledge your biggest assets, they will also be disguised from all of us.

8. Live it up.
Take a chance on life. Try a new activity. Though it takes you 5 hours to complete a half-marathon, play, dance, or speak up for what is right. Your physical and emotional well-being can be improved by embracing the little pleasures in life. In contrast, optimism draws positive things, whereas negativity produces negativity.

9. Develop A Mindfulness Practice.

Leave your hands on your tummy and try focusing just on your breathing for a few minutes. Even if you get sidetracked, gradually bring your attention back to your breathing. Your focus and self-control will return once you've exercised your attention muscles and blocked out the stresses of daily life.

8.4 7 ADHD RELAXATION TRICKS

At work, at home, on the way to school, at the PTA meeting, and a slew of other places.

1. Accept Your ADHD

Stop blaming yourself when you forget to do something or are late for something. ADHD is a neurobiological disorder, and it will not go away. You should get proper treatment and diagnosis. If you have ADHD, join a support group in your area or on the Internet. Stress can be reduced simply by realizing it, but you're not alone.

2. Observe The Passing of Hours and Minutes.

As a result of their condition, many people with ADHD see time as an abstract concept. Buy a wristwatch with a chime and set it to ring every hour to better keep track of time. Get a countdown timer that rings after 5 minutes if you always need "just 5 more minutes."

Eventually, you'll find yourself struggling to meet deadlines, and with perseverance, you'll learn how to properly manage your time.

3. Consider Your Alternatives

Exercising is a powerful stress-busting tool. Serotonin levels in the brain are improved by physical activity, which counteracts the effects of the stress hormone cortisol. The results of 30 minutes of exercise might last for 80 to 130 minutes, according to studies. Over time, exercise improves your ability to handle stress, allowing you to manage it more effectively.

4. Put Limits on Yourself
Scheduling too much time in advance can cause anxiety. When you're stressed, you're more likely to be impulsive or have an internal voice that tells you, "I should do X, Y, and Z." 3 times a day, say "no." Ask yourself, "What am I saying 'no' to?" each time you say "yes." Relaxation? In the mood for a tune?

5. Keep Your Guard Up
A lot of women fall into a false sense of safety once they've made a few improvements and then give up the strategies that helped them get there. ADHD sufferers frequently forget they have the disorder. Keep your wits about you!

6. Take a Break and Have Fun
You're exhausting yourself at risk for burnout if you don't take pauses from today's hectic lifestyle. Make time for fun in your schedule. Every week, meet together with pals for supper or a movie. Take a weekend getaway to the country or the beach. Find something you're passionate about and go after it without a second thought.

7. Get to Know Structure and Use It to Your Advantage
A structure can be helpful for those who have a hard time adhering to it, even for those with ADHD. Two ways I've found to be really helpful for me: Before you go to sleep, make a goal list of what you want to do the following day. You'll feel more centered when you wake up. Set a constant bedtime and wake-up time every single day. As a result, your circadian rhythms are more likely to be stabilized, resulting in better quality sleep.

CHAPTER 9: MINDFULNESS FOR ADHD

ADHD Sufferers Can Benefit From Mindfulness, But How Does It Work?

In contrast to many ADHD therapies, mindfulness focuses on improving a person's inner abilities. Using this technique can help you better control your concentration by helping you build your capacity to watch yourself, train your focus, and develop new attitudes to stressful circumstances. You learn to focus on the process of paying attention, and it can also help people become more conscious of their emotional condition; so they don't impulsively respond when faced with a difficult situation. For those with ADHD, this is a common source of frustration.

Meditation for ADHD has been talked about for a long time, but the concern was always whether persons with ADHD, predominantly hyperactive ones, could actually perform it. It is possible to tailor mindfulness to suit your own needs because of its adaptability and versatility.

Can I learn to cultivate mindfulness on my own?

Yes, the fundamentals are straightforward. Spend 5 minutes concentrating on the feeling of inhaling and exhaling and how your stomach goes up and down as you do so, in a quiet place where you won't be disturbed. As time goes on, you'll begin to notice that you're thinking about something else—whether it's your job, the noise you just heard, or your plans for the rest of the day. Take a deep breath and label these emotions as "thinking."

Continually engage in this mindfulness routine. Every day, increase the amount of time you spend doing the exercise—10 minutes, 15 minutes, up to 20 minutes if possible. Spend a few minutes or a few times a day focusing on your breath, whether you're staying from one location to another, sitting at a stop sign, or working at a computer.

Even in the middle of a conversation, you can cultivate a state of mindfulness. Even if it's just for a few minutes at a time, it's a terrific way to practice mindfulness. Let go of your busy thoughts and focus on what's going on right now in your daily life because that's what it's all about.

9.1 ADHD SYMPTOM RELIEF WITH MINDFULNESS MEDITATION

There are two constant everyday obstacles for people with ADHD: paying close attention and sustaining self-regulation. Because of this, it follows that a form of concentration training that also improves one's ability to regulate one's impulses would be an excellent natural treatment for ADHD.

What is "mindful awareness?"
Various religious traditions practice mindful meditation or mindfulness. Vipassana meditation, for example, can be found in Buddhist teachings.

Meditation is not, however, a religion or a spiritual practice. In other words, it's about becoming more aware of your ideas, feelings, and physiological sensations. It can be utilized as a means to promote health and well-being, particularly in terms of mental health, decrease blood pressure, and manage stress, chronic pain, and mood problems.

ADHD Meditation for the Restless and Bored
Stress and worry in an overactive ADHD mind can be reduced by orienting one's focus to the present moment, improving mood, and completing an efficient ADHD treatment plan.

The rise in the notoriety of mindfulness has inevitably led to certain misunderstandings about what it is and how it works. Mindfulness can help adults with ADHD overcome their problems and lower their levels of anxiety and stress.

Step # 1: Practice Mindful Labeling
Mindfulness can be introduced into your daily routine by taking a few minutes to observe your thoughts and feelings. This can be conducted as part of a regular meditation routine (for example, by taking 5–10 minutes to sit quietly and contemplate your surroundings) or at random times during

the day.

To begin, pay attention to and name (i.e., label) your thoughts, feelings, and physical reactions to give a response to a stressful event or situation. This can help you separate yourself from the thoughts that come to you automatically.

"I'm terribly worried," you can say out loud or in your thinking. I'm struggling and feeling overburdened right now." Take a moment to observe any tension in your muscles, especially in the shoulders and jaws. Look for signs of stress, such as a beating heart or perspiration. Any feelings and thoughts should be observed, even concerning self-judgment thoughts.

Being able to do this kind of "tuning in" with compassion and love is critical, mainly when anxiety is at its worst.

Step # 2: Redirect Your Focus
Trying to weaken the link between worry and becoming consumed by it is the next step after you've acknowledged that you're experiencing an anxious state of mind. This is where mindfulness and attention training come in.

Take a break from worrying by shifting your focus to something else. It is possible to accomplish as follows:

Focusing on the feelings of the breath, rather than worrying about the "thought fog," is the primary goal of breathing exercises. By focusing on the breath, you can often relax your body as well. This is especially true if you take your time to breathe slowly and fully exhale. In the event that you find yourself drifting away from the breath, don't worry; just keep returning. Breathwork can be practiced in a variety of ways, including:

- Paying attention to your natural breathing cycle. This may be sufficient to put concern in perspective.

- When practicing "box breathing," inhale, pause, and then

exhale every four counts.

- Hand on the belly, using feeling at hand to anchor focus and facilitate respiration from the base, not the chest.
- Using words like "in" and "out" when breathing and "out" when exhaling can help you stay focused.
- For example, envision a wave of peaceful energy coming into your body as you inhale and a sea of stress going out when you exhale.

Informal activities

· Taking a walk-in nature

· Playing an instrument

· Drinking hot tea

· Listening to music

· Exercising

· Put something cold on your eyes.

· Writing down thoughts

· Praying

· Taking a relaxing supplement

Step 3: Take a Look Back at the Situation
Once you've regained some control over your anxiety, go back to the circumstance that initially sparked it so you may reflect on what went wrong and take any necessary action. Developing this kind of self-awareness allows you to be present at the moment without succumbing to the emotion it evokes. More information is now available, allowing you to get to the bottom of your worry and the sentiments that lie underlying it.

While you're in this state, consider these suggestions:

- What made me fearful?

- Why am I concerned about the current state of affairs?

- Am I thinking in ways that are counterproductive to my goals? For example, blaming yourself or imagining the worst possible outcomes.

- Is it possible for me to deal with this fear or anxiety? How? Otherwise, how can I develop the ability to cope with and thrive in an uncertain world?

Step 4: Self-Coaching can be learned

Developing a positive and ADHD-informed internal voice is an integral part of self-coaching, as it aids in recognizing what is required at any given time and how to work through concerns and problems. The following is what this inner voice tells me to do:

- caring for one another and checking on one's emotions

- slowing down and paying enough attention to your own body pacing

- self-accountability and a willingness to take responsibility for one's own challenges with attention deficit

What is most essential to you right now, this month, this year, or this phase of your life?

Practicing mindfulness makes it easier. As humans, we aren't wired to always live in the present moment. When it comes to analytical, creative, or planning thinking, our propensity to become caught up in our thoughts is an asset. Being able to take a deep breath, observe your reaction, and analyze your options can be a game-changer in times of stress.

CHAPTER 10: ADHD & RELATIONSHIPS

As a result of having ADHD, you may have difficulty communicating with your closest friends and family members. There are, however, the best strategies to improve your relationships.

It might be difficult to function when you're constantly being reprimanded, nagged, and micromanaged by others who have ADHD. It doesn't matter what you do; your partner or spouse doesn't appear to like it. You find yourself ignoring your companion or stating whatever you have to get them off your back since you don't feel appreciated as an adult. You wish your partner would relax a little and quit attempting to dominate every aspect of your existence. When you first met the guy you fell in love with, you wondered what had happened to them.

People with ADHD can make another person feel uncomfortable and unappreciated; if you're dating someone with this condition, you may feel fed up with being the one who has to take care of everything in the relationship. You don't trust your partner; he's often totally disinterested, can't hold up his end of the bargain, and you're forced to remind him of his promises or do the work yourself.

10.1 FRIENDSHIPS

People with ADHD have great difficulty developing and maintaining long-term friendships due to the symptoms of the disorder. Those with ADHD generally struggle to acquire social skills; they have difficulty with attention, impulsivity, and mood regulation.

For example, your inability to pay attention or your impulsivity might be misinterpreted by your peers as shyness or hostility.

A Guide for Women with ADHD on How to Make Friends
When a woman is accepted by her peers, she feels more confident about herself. They are characterized by the intensity of their bonds.

Women with ADHD have some of the most challenging and distressing difficulties when it comes to social relationships.

The idea that for women is always easier to establish relationships is a misconception. Women with ADHD try to cover up their social difficulties; fear of being exposed as fraudulent keeps them from making acquaintances.

Communication, active listening, and a keen eye for nonverbal clues are necessary for healthy friendships to flourish. This skill set is complex for the majority of ADHD-afflicted women to maintain over time.

Women with ADHD: Social Strategies
- **Acknowledge Your Thought Processes**

You can't change your brain or the way the world expects you to act. That being said, you can see that the truth we perceive has been molded by our perspective. But you have the ability to reduce the influence that expectations have over your life by altering your perspective on their significance.

The ideal thing is to see the world through the eyes of someone who understands and appreciates your particular set of circumstances. You may focus on your strengths instead of apologizing for your weaknesses when you are freed from social limitations and judgments. You can balance your own needs by appreciating your own values rather than those of society.

Making and maintaining friendships that nourish you can be easier if you have empathy for your difficulties.

- **Utilize Technology to Help Manage Your ADHD**

The use of brain technology can make it easier to socialize. Friends want to be acknowledged, but they don't require it to be sent via postal mail.

When it comes to remembering significant dates, you may rely on pop-up notifications and alarms.

If you pay close attention to your alarms, you can gain control over your life. When you say, "I'll do that in a minute," your mind is free to work on something else. Stop using the "snooze" feature on your alarms and make a conscious effort to get up whenever the alarm goes off. Procrastination isn't an option when you're standing.

The silence is broken and appreciated by a one-line text. It's best to set an alarm that goes off at the moment you need to leave, rather than the moment you're meeting for lunch. Don't forget that need time will take to get to your destination if you don't want to be rushed.

- **Consider Your ADHD Triggers in Advance.**

Be conscious of any red flags in your life. Women with attention deficit hyperactivity disorder (ADHD) have a hard time playing a team role. They believe that their peculiarities make them ineligible to join clubs or committees. It is not uncommon for women with ADHD to become irritable and disengaged in social situations, as their brains are always searching for new stimuli.

Sit in the middle of the table if you're having a group dinner. Individuals on both sides allow you to switch discussions if you lose interest in a topic. Respect your brain's need to move on when you start to stifle a yawn, fidget, or check the clock. Rest and recharge your batteries in the bathroom. Take a walk, check your phone, and see if you can come back with an excuse to depart early.

- **Openly Discuss Your Symptoms of ADHD**

Spend time with people who understand your differences and are willing to accommodate them. A few of my pals need quick attention, and any delay is seen as a sign of neglect. "I'm not good at replying, but your emails are precious to me," you can say without apologies. When I get back to you, I promise. It's essential to consider the emotional and psychological expenses of a friendship while deciding whether or not to keep it.

- **Consider if Incorporating Shopping into Your Plans**

Replace a shopping trip with a walk or lunch date. It's not uncommon for women with ADHD to find it difficult to shop with other ladies. A multi-sensory setting is essential for their success.

It's difficult for women with ADHD to provide care for the needs of others when they have attention deficit hyperactivity disorder (ADHD). Many of them agree to go shopping on the spur of the moment, but then they're not ready to go when the time arrives. "Shopping's not my strong point" is the better way to go about it when establishing arrangements. "How about going for a walk or having lunch?"

10.2 LOVE & SEXUALITY

Orgasm is commonly a problem for women with ADHD. Some women claim to be able to have numerous orgasms in a short period of time, while others claim that even after lengthy stimulation, they are unable to achieve orgasm.

Individuals with ADHD may be more sensitive. To put it another way, a sexual activity that is pleasurable for a partner who does not suffer from ADHD may be distressing for the individual with the disorder.

An individual with ADHD may find the smells, sensations, and tastes common in sexual encounters unattractive or irritating. Intimacy can be difficult for somebody with ADHD because of their hyperactivity. Having a partner with ADHD can make it difficult to relax enough to get in the mood for intimacy.

How ADHD Impacts Marriage and Sex
Trust, connection, and commitment are the building blocks of a long-term partnership like marriage. Most marriages start off with the best of intentions. After that, reality sets in, and everything gets a little messed up. Inattention, impulsivity, and lack of executive function are daily obstacles for women with ADHD and also have a significant impact on relationships and dating life.

In this case, "Mixed marriage" is one in which one partner has been diagnosed with ADHD, and the other has not. Usually, the non-ADHD partner talks about their difficulties because of their partner's inability to get things done, forgetfulness, impulsivity, intense emotions like anger, and issues with communication, and unrealistic expectations to consider.

- 41% of women with ADHD indicated that their sex life was influenced "a lot" by the condition's symptoms.
- Non-ADHD partners, on the other hand, frequently

complained of sexual unhappiness due to altered marital roles.

- You may want a variety of partners to have sex with. Casual sex is risky and is more probable if sexual intimacy in a long-term relationship is disrupted. As a result, partners reported feeling physically and emotionally rejected, making it impossible for them to have sex.

- Risky actions, such as unprotected sex, may be attractive to you. Neurotransmitters, which are substances in the brain, can be reduced in people with ADHD. That could make you more prone to taking chances or being impulsive, which can be dangerous.

- The link between ADHD and intense emotions, particularly rage, was commonly recognized as the love-killer.

- Stress, distraction, medication side effects, or misaligned sex drives were indicated as the most common causes of sex life disruptions for partners with ADHD. Discord was exacerbated by disputes over the most typical symptoms of ADHD.

How Couples Make Things Work in the Real World

- Speak your mind, but don't overdo it. If being caressed continuously bothers you, make sure to instruct your partner on how and when to do so. This can help avoid misunderstandings and disagreements.

- If your partner notices that you're easily distracted or easily irritated because of your ADHD, you must tell them. It isn't their fault, and they should know that.

- Eliminate sources of distraction. Wanting to have sex in the dark might help you stay focused if you tend to drift off during the act of sexual intimacy with a partner.

- Intimacy, not sex, should be the focus. Orgasm may be

more difficult if you have difficulty concentrating. Spend time on other acts of intimacy besides intercourse, such as kissing and foreplay. This alleviates some of the stress and allows you and your spouse to have a good time together.

- Maintain a healthy level of physical activity. Dopamine is a neurotransmitter associated with well-being and pleasure, which can be increased with regular physical activity. You'll be able to appreciate closeness more and be less inclined to participate in unsafe sexual practices due to this.

- Follow the directions of your medical prescriptions carefully. Drugs that treat ADHD can either increase your sexual drive or decrease your capacity to concentrate and have fun during sex. In this case, have a discussion about it with your specialist and your spouse.

- Consider a talk therapy session. According to research, talk therapy has been shown to reduce the symptoms of ADHD that interfere with your sexual life. Additionally, the therapist can help you and your spouse improve your communication both in and out of the bedroom.

10.3 PARENTING

Women are more likely to find out about their ADHD later in life when they are mothers than when they were kids. The main reason is that ADHD manifests itself differently in both sexes. Women are more likely than men to suffer from the inattentive form of ADHD instead of the hyperactive/impulsive or mixed forms. These girls may have been habitually disorganized and underachieved in high school, but they were often neglected because they were less likely to disrupt the classroom.

ADHD Women Are Being Crushed by the Myth of Motherhood

- ADHD moms have to deal with poor working memory, executive dysfunction, and emotional sensitivity on top of their difficulties.

- Mothers are held to unrealistic and unhealthy standards by society.

- In addition, their children are often affected by ADHD as well.

However, most women work tirelessly to be "excellent mothers"—and end up exhausted, depressed, or lost as a result.

Every aspect of parenting, even the typical "how to be a good mother" roadmap, needs to be re-examined if you have ADHD.

Moms with ADHD: How to Survive

- **Don't stop what you're doing to answer a call**

You begin activity A, only to put it aside in favor of task B, which you soon realize is equally essential. Task C suddenly appears on your radar. This sounds familiar? Follow the rule of "Don't stop one errand with another." If this is the case, finish the previous one before moving on to the following tasks. Don't forget to write down the other assignment that came to mind at the last minute.

- **Relax and take it easy at the beginning of the day**

The 15 minutes you have before you need to get up can be used to meditate, check your list of things to do, and organize your thoughts.

- **Even if you're at home, get a babysitter.**

If your kid is hyperactive, a college or high school student might be a support system. As an inattentive ADHD sufferer, you may find it difficult to keep up with an energetic child, especially those living in an active household.

- **Set up a snare and a barricade**

Get everything you need for the next day before you go to sleep: to-do list, keys, briefcase, and letters to mail. Put them on a stool in front of the door so that they block your way.

Alternatively, you can hang a basket full of essentials near the front door for easy access. Using a hanger string, attach the other end to the doorknob.

- **Meal timings should be flexible**

Even deciding what to eat for supper might be a challenge. Overfeeding your children isn't worth developing a stomachache. Hyperactive children should be let roam around on their own. You and your family will enjoy a more pleasant dining experience, and your kids will eat more as a result.

- **Hire a teacher**

If the mother's ADHD medication wears out at the same time as the child's, she may not have the patience to assist with homework. A couple of days a week, hire a high school kid who can help relieve some of your stress. You'll have a better time relaxing in the evenings.

- **Posting timetables**

Make sure everyone can see the calendar for the following week by placing it in a prominent area. Everyone will be able to see exactly where everyone else is heading and what doing in a matter of seconds. As a result, there will be misunderstandings and less tense situations, less embarrassment, and interruptions.

- **Make use of visual cues**

Items should be color-coded so that they may be quickly identified as yours and not someone else's.

- **Make no more promises**

Make promises to your kids that you know you can keep, and your life will be a lot less stressful. Only by saying, "We'll see how it goes," can you approach making a commitment. Go ahead and try to do something nice for someone if the opportunity presents itself. Keep your options open, but don't get tethered down to anything.

CHAPTER 11: HOME ORGANIZATION

With ADHD, staying on top of one's to-do list is a major issue. Clutter is a problem for many individuals, and it can make them feel stuck or overwhelmed in their professional and personal lives.

11.1 CLUTTER

13 Clutter-busting Tips for People Who Get Overwhelmed Easily

If you find it challenging to complete a single chore, such as washing dishes or folding laundry. Set a stopwatch for 15 minutes and stick to your task until the stopwatch goes off; it can be reset if you think you can continue.

1. Mail Must Be Handled on a Regular Basis

Every day, collect and sort your mail to avoid a buildup of paper. Make sure you have a recycling can near your desk or the entrance so that you may get rid of unwanted mail before it reaches your work area and clutters it. Correspondence should be categorized according to the action it needs to be taken. Use a specific folder or inbox to keep track of the most urgent documents.

2. Prevent Clutter from Building up in the First Place

Make tables and dressers less attractive if you have a tendency to amass clutter there. Set the table after you've cleaned up the dining room. As well as being aesthetically pleasing, the dining table is no longer a place where clutter can accumulate. Your bedside table should be filled with photos or memories in the same way as your desk.

3. Keep Relevant Things Together

Organize frequently used objects together. That way, you don't have to constantly rush around to find the supplies you need to complete a task. As a bonus, you won't have to go out and buy duplicates. For example, put all of your gift-wrapping supplies in the same place, such as in a closet.

4. Label Storage Containers

To lighten the load, you can adopt the mantra "out of sight, out of mind" when things are sorted and packed. Keeping a record of your things is easier if they are stored in the same containers. To keep track of what's in the box, attach cards to the sides and update them when needed. When you put the container away, make sure the label is facing out so you can see what's inside.

5. Create a Task File
Adult women with ADHD have a hard time keeping up with their daily chores. Having a weekly plan can help you stay on target. Calendars are an optimal way to keep track of all the tasks that need to be completed in the following week. Keep them all in one place, arranged according to importance. If you live with a partner or spouse, speak about what each of you is going to do and make a decision together.

6. Make Junk Drawers a Specialty
Unmarked orphan screws and CDs can impede down decluttering efforts by making it difficult to find new homes for them. Keep at least 1 junk drawer across every room to avoid this. Keep it in the drawer if you don't have any idea where to put it; organize the contents of the drawer once it's full to the brim. Use what you can and get rid of what you can't. Begin the process again.

7. It's time to Hire a Clutter Buddy
Sort your junk into 4 piles: "keep," "trash," 'donation' and 'age' at least once a year with the help of your best friend or a professional organizer. The "toss" goods should be thrown away as soon as possible—before you have an opportunity to reconsider. Items that can be donated should be placed in a donation bin nearby. Three months later, review the "age" items that you've saved. Make a note on your calendar so don't miss the event and repeat it.

8. Eliminate the Root Cause of Clutter
In order to keep your closet from becoming cluttered, you

should establish a rule: If you bring in 2 new pairs of shoes, you must get rid of one old pair. All home products are subject to the same rule.

When shopping at a thrift store or yard sale, put your hands in your pockets to avoid carrying unwanted items home. Buying anything is linked to how you feel about it when you touch it.

9. Organize the Magazines and Newspaper You Don't Read Into a Single Location

Put unread magazines in a small basket if they tend to accumulate. Create a mental inventory of what you have and what you don't need. If you can't get through all of it, throw it away or recycle it. Alternatively, you may drop off a few of the top magazines at a women's shelter or hospital.

If you can't keep up with an issue of a magazine on a regular basis, consider canceling your membership or reading it online instead.

10. Declutter Your Home with This Fun Game

Try this trick if you're stuck with the sheer volume of clutter in a room: Cover most of the junk you want to organize with a sheet or blanket, allowing you to see only one area at a time. The chaos you can see should be sorted. Once you've sorted the first section, turn the sheet over to uncover more clutter and sort it out.

11. Technology Stuff Should Be Reined in

There is a new clutter for many persons with ADHD: computers and electronic devices. You should appoint a "device captain" to keep track of all gadgets, make sure old ones are disposed of properly, and that all cables are tagged and stored.

12. Streamline Your Finances and Pay Your Bills More Efficiently

A personal checking account and online banking are the best ways to save money. You may reduce paper clutter by paying all of your bills automatically.

Ask your accountant if monthly bank statements are necessary. It's possible that you can get away with just keeping quarterly or annual reports.

13. In a Series of Bursts, Straighten Up

If you find it challenging to complete a single chore, such as washing dishes or folding laundry, try breaking it up into smaller, more manageable chunks. Set a timer for 15 minutes and stick to your task until the timer goes off. The timer can be reset if you believe you can keep going.

11.2 MANAGE YOUR HOUSE

Shortcuts to a Less Cluttered, Cleaner House
"House arrest" or "Housekeeping": Which is more appropriate? ADHD sufferers, in particular, may have difficulty distinguishing between the two.

Straightening Up
If you have a hard time remembering what you need to do with a specific item, it may assist if you keep it out in the open. Clutter, on the other hand, is unsightly and distracting. A painless approach to get rid of chaos would be greatly appreciated by me. However, it does need a fair amount of time and effort. But if you follow a plan, things will go more smoothly.

Use clear, labeled containers, boxes, and baskets to keep things out of view but not out of mind. When a box is full, it's time to look through it and get rid of stuff you don't need.

Once you're in one room, walk on to the next one to your right. Repeat this action until you return to your starting point. As you travel from room to room, keep a plastic bag handy. The trash bag holds everything you don't want to keep. Throw out old magazines and trash mail but don't waste your time sorting through loose papers. It's time to get on with the rest of your day. When you have more time, come back and read them.

Dusting a table, desk, or another surface can begin once you've cleared enough space for a shift. Chairs and sofas deserve special consideration. Whenever I see a customer, I tell them, "You deserve to sit in this chair all to yourself."

Toss anything that doesn't belong in the room you're in toward the door. Go outside and pick it up on your way out. Then, resume to your rightward circle.

Tossing and Turning

- Even if your kitchen is constructed of marble and gold, a dirty sink and a muddy backsplash will ruin the aesthetics.

- Use a "clean/dirty" sign to indicate when the dishwasher needs to be run. Turn on the dishwasher and wash the dinnerware once you've finished eating. Unload the clean plates and cutlery the following day. Wait to run the dishwasher after rinsing and loading the breakfast dishes. Rinse the dinnerware, put it in the dishwasher, and on it after dinner. Every day, go through the same motions.

- Take a whiff every time you open the fridge and throw out anything that smells off. Once a month, thoroughly clean the refrigerator. Paper towels are preferable to sponges because they are less likely to become infected. Paper towels in droves. Using a dry paper towel, wipe up any liquids that have been spilled. Use a moist paper towel if the object is dry, such as crumbs.

- A sponge should only be used for seven days before being washed in the dishwasher and re-used. Throw it away after that.

- Furniture spray is not recommended for use on wood—none of it works. Instead, use a cloth that has been gently dampened.

- About once a week, clean the floors and wipe down the counters. To clean, just move all the stuff first to the right, then to the left and repeat the process. It's time to declutter if you can't even move around the room because there is too much junk.

Doing Laundry

- Get a large basket for darks and a smaller one for whites and separate them. Have your family members put their soiled clothing directly into these 2 communal baskets instead than in hampers.

- When the hampers are full, put the clothing in the washer and set two timers to ensure that you actually do the laundry. Leave one on top of the dryer and carry the other about the house as you complete extra laundry-related duties. As an example, this includes making beds, folding linens, matching socks, ironing, as well as other tasks. After each load is done, throw it in the dryer, set your alarms, and start doing more laundry.

- Doing the laundry once a week will require at least three 40-minute blocks of time or 2 hours of work each time.

Cleaning Bathrooms
- You should take a hot shower once a week and close the bathroom door. You'll have a good start on cleaning, thanks to the steam.

- Use glass cleaner to clean the mirrors, while a non-glass cleaner is used to clean the countertops. Paper towels work well for this. Clean the floor before you leave.

- Isn't cleaning something you're in the mood for? Put on a favorite playlist, sip a cappuccino, or belt out a song of your choice. Turning on the TV will be too distracting, so don't do it. You can make it a challenge to see how much activity you can get by wearing an electronic pedometer. You're off!

- Housekeeping chores may not always be completed to your satisfaction. In the end, the work must get done on time.

- A fictional visit from a bachelor brother should be enough to keep your house spotless. Your home doesn't need to be immaculate until your mother is actually in town.

11.3 MEAL PLANNING

Say Goodbye to the "What's For Dinner?" Stress
Are you feeling frustrated when it comes to meal planning and preparation? This ADHD-friendly system may help alleviate some of your burdens. You'll be able to get the meal on the dining table in an instant, thanks to these simple meal plans.

- Organize a gathering of the family. Dinnertime is a great time for this. Ask your loved ones to recommend their favorite meal recipes to you. The healthy equilibrium of each meal suggested by children must be taken into consideration, even if their tastes are considered.

- Create a "Top 10" list of the best dinners. Over the course of 2 weeks, you'll cook these dinners, leaving two nights a week free for takeout or ordering in.

- Individual index cards can be used to list all of the elements of a dish, as well as its ingredients.

- Organize your meal cards in a way that saves you time at the office. For example, make a couple of extra chicken breasts on Thursday evening to use in your chicken Caesar Salad for the next two days.

- The index cards should always be accessible. Use paper clips to organize them into 2 groups of 5, and you'll be ready to buy whenever the time comes.

- In just six simple steps, you'll have all of your meals scheduled and the rest of your grocery list typed out.

- Refresh the menu. If you and your family have become tired of the top 10 dinner meals you came up with, have a meeting to solicit new ideas.

- Dinner preparations should be shared among the family members. Each night of the week, designate a "cook assigned" for that night. As a "cook's assistant," younger children can help out by preparing the table, gathering supplies, and doing other tasks. Middle or high school students can learn one or two of the top 10 family dinners. When it comes to cooking for their loved ones, they may actually embrace the task.

Grocery Shopping Tips

No, they are not designed to make us feel anxious. Particularly for those of us with ADHD, a seemingly primary weekly task may rapidly become mind-boggling due to packed aisles, confusing pricing, and tempting displays. To prevent overspending, stick to your budget, and quickly get in and out of the store, follow these shopping hacks.

- **With a Pencil Attached, Post Your Shopping List**

If you want to keep your lists on paper, display them where everyone can see them every day, such as on the fridge. If you're running out on something, write it down as soon as you realize it.

- **Tech It Up**

With the help of some smartphone apps, the supermarket shopping experience has taken a significant step ahead. Make a list and share it with your family and friends using an online app that makes it simple to add items.

- **Be Aware of the Shop**

Do the same thing every time you go shopping. Don't sabotage your brain's efforts to learn the layout so that you can find items more quickly in the future.

- **Don't Go Grocery Shopping Hungry**

You're more prone to buy things on impulse if your blood glucose is low. Before going shopping, make sure you've eaten something since this can help alleviate your frustration and ensure that you don't buy goods you don't actually need just because they seem promising!

- **Designate a Day for Shopping**

Shop at the same time, once a week, to avoid impulsive purchases. Take advantage of a weekday morning or evening to avoid crowds. Avoid trying to go before or after work on weekdays and go before your child's soccer practice ends if you can.

- **Purchase in Advance**

Don't wait until a lasting minute to buy non-perishables like canned products or toilet paper. In the event that one of your three toilet paper packets is used, get a new one immediately. To prevent the hassle of running out of paper towels, you'll stock up ahead of time!

- **Make a Cash Payment**

Make an advance list of everything you will need and then estimate the cost of each item on the list. Each week, decide on a spending limit and take that money out before you go to the store. There's no chance of overspending because you can't buy things without paying for them.

CHAPTER 12: MONEY & BUDGETS

New year, new life! And we are ready. Create a new financial record-keeping strategy for individuals with ADHD by turning over a new leaf. Adults with attention deficit hyperactivity disorder (ADHD) will not be able to use many financial management systems because they take too much time, paper, and attention to detail. Is there anything that can be done? Consistency and simplicity.

Track Spending

- Keeping tabs on our daily expenditures is one of the most critical financial chores we face. Don't worry; I'm not suggesting you maintain a log of every single purchase of chewing gum. Instead of keeping track of how much money you spend, keep an eye on your wallet.

- Here's how it all works: Decide how much you can possibly spend each week on non-essentials like movies, video rentals, coffee, and incidentals by looking at your monthly budget. That sum is your weekly stipend in dollars. You should withdraw your weekly allowance from your ATM the same day each week. When it comes to weekend spending, Friday is a great day. Every time you go out, you'll know what your weekly budget exactly is and whether you can afford it. Just take a look at your wallet's cash supply.

- Make your own lunches and skip Starbucks if you spent too much money over the weekend because a quick look at your wallet will tell you. Don't worry about keeping track of anything; just adhere to your decision to stay away from ATM until Friday.

Pay Bills Online
- There hasn't been a more ADHD-friendly innovation in a long time. After a short setup, you'll be able to pay all your bills electronically. Your monthly bills can be paid automatically, so you don't have to worry about lost envelopes or late fees, and you may log on whenever you need to pay other more unusual invoices.

- It's best to set up an auto-payment that is marginally higher than your average monthly balance to have enough money to settle all the bills. You'll be able to pay a larger-than-average charge as your credit improves over time.

Prepare for Taxes
- A plastic folder case with a handle is the best way to keep track of everything you'll need for your tax return, particularly your monthly receipt slips. Do the same for all tax-related documents that arrive in the mail.

- Hanging files, such as those for tax-deductible donations and expenses for business, housing, and childcare, might help you stay more organized.

- Get a consultation with a professional to find out what receipts you need to keep. Instead of piling tax documents in a jumble on a desk or table, it's critical to select one accessible place to store them.

Save for Retirement
- Making savings a habit is the most effective approach to putting money aside for the future. The much money a person has saved, the more likely they are to keep it in savings, and the less likely they are to put money in savings if they have to take action. It's a straightforward matter.

- Set up an automated monthly transfer of money from

your checking account to a money or savings market account through your bank. The same hands-off approach can be used to invest in both mutual funds and stocks.

12.1 THE MONEY-SAVING TIPS FOR PEOPLE WITH ADHD

The average American family saves about 1% to 2% of their income, and those with attention deficit disorder (ADHD) have an even more difficult time preparing for the future. Here's a step-by-step method to ultimately get out of debt, reduce your monthly expenditures, and spend less.

- **Be Conscious of Your Spending**

You should first focus on living within your means, which means no more expenditures on credit cards.

- **Credit Cards with low-interest rates**

Use 0% or poor credit cards to consolidate your consumer debt. Paying less each month means that the interest rate is lower. Customers with strong credit are more likely to receive these deals, but you can also locate them on the Internet.

- **Make a Payment with a Credit Card**

Your funded credit card should be stored somewhere that is safe but difficult to access. It's possible to give your card to a member of your family. Make it clear that you will only ask for it in the event of a real emergency. Another alternative is to keep the card in a deposit box in your bank. As an alternative, freeze the card in ice cubes in your freezer to make it more durable. In time, you will know whether or not a potential purchase is necessary or merely a whim to satisfy your urges.

- **Try out online banking**

Online banking can be used to set up recurring monthly payments. Make sure your credit card transaction is always on time by setting up a payment reminder. Register for online bill payment at your bank's website and open an account. After that, you can set up recurring monthly fees for other debts. A mortgage payment and payments to phone and utility companies should be included in these invoices because they are predictable expenses.

- **Begin Saving Now**

Use your zero-interest or low-interest rate credit card to save money while you pay down your balance. Checking frequently this credit card, your debt, and your budget are all ways to see how much money you're saving. This amount should be put aside for the future. Have your bank automatically transfer that amount each week into two savings accounts: one for an emergency fund, the other for retirement.

- **Make Better Purchasing Decisions When You Shop**

Avoid the mall by making a list of the things you need and just going to the places where they're on sale. The easiest way to avoid online purchasing is simply not bookmarking any of your favorite sites. Forget about purchasing, and instead, use the Internet as a place to learn.

- **Stop Wasting So Much Money**

When it comes to fixing a budget, most people, especially those with ADHD, are apprehensive about the process. Simply estimating how much money you don't have is a tedious and disheartening task. You don't have to go through the agony of creating a personal financial plan that you can work with.

- **Don't spend more money than you earn**

What is the secret to a successful budget? Spend less than the sum of your earnings. It may sound straightforward, but it actually needs a lot of rigorous financial record keeping, which isn't one of our strong points. Keep a running tally of everything your purchases for a month. Record all of your transactions and print out invoices for internet purchases as soon as feasible.

- **Decide on a spending limit**

Start with defining "budgeting" and why you need it in your life. Assume that you dislike the word and be truthful with yourself about it. It's time to rethink your approach to budgeting and see it as a vital step that will allow you to plan for the future and not worry about bills. When you pay your bills, put up a list of 10 compelling reasons why you should develop healthy spending habits. Those with attention deficit hyperactivity disorder (ADHD) flourish when they have a well-defined plan of action. The following is a list of things you need to accomplish in regard to your finances.

- **In the end, you'll have learned a lot from your mistakes.**

Use a money notebook during your month of monitoring to enhance your awareness of your spending and to examine if each transaction is worth the money you are spending. Adults with attention deficit disorder (ADHD) are more likely to overspend during the holiday season. Nothing can be stopped by sheer willpower. As an alternative, write down who you're buying for and set a spending limit for the day. When you purchase something, write down how you feel about it.

- **Reducing the Costs**

Certain costs are, of course, pre-determined. It's time to look for places where you've been splurging on discretionary items. Have you purchased more books, even though your shelves are already overflowing? Have you bought new clothes, even though your closet is already bursting at the seams? What attracted you to our store? Alternatively, did you go berserk at the supermarket?

- **Establish a Spending Plan**

You'll now be required to disclose all of your monthly spending, both fixed and discretionary, in order to have a complete picture of where your money goes. Always have three times your disposable income in the bank as a backup plan in the event of a financial emergency. Then, take a moment to be grateful. You're not "going without" because your budget covers all of your basic necessities. To help you keep to your budget, incorporate some enjoyable spending as well.

- **If you don't have a contingency plan in place for unexpected expenses**

Regardless of how meticulously you plan, unforeseen occurrences and emergencies are likely to arise. This is accounted for in the finest budgets. Preventive steps can save you much money down the road. To keep your family healthy, see a doctor on a regular basis. Make sure your car and home are in working order with regular maintenance. Make sure you have enough money saved up in case something like this happens to you. Include it in your savings account.

CHAPTER 13: GETTING THINGS DONE

There are exceptional productivity and concentration skills for adults with ADHD that can help them get things done, even when their symptoms get in the way. Here are my favorites.

13.1 PRODUCTIVITY CAN BE ATTAINED BY TALKING

ADHD therapists and coaches advise people with ADHD to engage in "self-talk" in order to improve their lives. Considering that we speak to ourselves in the same way we would like others to talk to us, there is a tremendous deal of value in doing so. Unfortunately, this isn't the norm. Our memories and self-criticism are shaped by the 20% of our actions that went wrong, not the 80% of good actions.

Useless negative phrases
The negative phrases we use to describe ourselves or our behaviors are harmful. Isn't it better to realize that our brains are not wired to process negative statements? That's right: our brains don't distinguish positive from negative; NO isn't processed in the dark depths of the mind. Therefore, "I would not waste my time on the computer" is interpreted as "I will waste my time on the computer."

What baffles us most is how we continue to find ourselves in these black holes. By repeating these statements in the negative, we have convinced ourselves! No matter how often we say "I don't...", we are still ordering ourselves to do something we don't want to do. Subsequently, we chastise ourselves.

Consider the following instances regarding deadlines and consider how you communicate with yourself. Are you encouraging, or are you critical of yourself?

- No matter how much it pains me, I'm not going to leave this chair until I've written three pages.

- "Don't even consider it, you slacker – you'd better get your act together!"

- Everybody was correct – I never organized anything. Just apply yourself, I ask myself.

- When I try to concentrate, my thoughts are all over the board. The task at hand will never be completed by me!

- God, I'm antsy; I'm so bored. I'd really like to go outdoors, but I'm unable to do so because I started this project a little late.

The reality is that your ADHD mind does not perform well when under stress. The place where new ideas are sown and nurtured, the creative well, runs dry. It's not a bad thing that you have a wandering mind but make an effort to direct your thoughts in a specific direction.

These types of self-talk can help you cope with looming deadlines:

- Two hours of writing time is allotted for today. No matter how much work I get done, I'm going to stop there.

- As far as I'm concerned, that deadline is 'dead."If I'm late, I'll inquire as to what will happen. I'll reassess my commitment if I can't show up on time. Is this something I genuinely want to do?"

- "This may not be the best time to put on paper all the ideas floating around in my head. I'll try again later."

- "This project is boring me to tears. Going for a walk outside sounds like a good idea to me. Tossing ideas around in a new environment will help me come up with new ones."

You may expect an amazing piece of literature from this "brain soup" at some point. Talking to oneself in the same way you might talk to a loved one works. You'll do more in less time and with less stress if you don't mortify yourself. After a little while, you might still grow to assume that all of those lovely things are true; you just don't know it at first.

13.2 FOR THOSE WITH ADHD STUCK ON TASKS

Not women with ADHD can be counted on to be as productive as the rest of women. Planning in advance is a weakness of ours. However, this does not imply that we are unable to accomplish our goals; we simply need to adopt a different mindset. For those like us with attention deficit disorder (ADHD), the following productivity techniques may not fit into a typical time management book.

- **Don't worry about being perfect**

Do not expect perfection from yourself. Focusing on getting better at work can lead to frustrating or letting the laundry pile up. Give yourself some wiggle room because you're human too.

- **Keep Your Eyes on the Prize**

Recognize that everything will take far longer than you expect. To avoid going berserk about missing your own deadline, make sure you have contingency plans in place, constantly imagining what you will get from your efforts, your "reason why."

- **Take part in a Scavenger Search**

Build a foundation of success. Before sitting down, make sure what you need is within reach, so you don't have to disrupt your concentration to get it later. You'll be glad to have a reason to quit what you're doing, I promise. In the beginning, remove that option.

- **Allow Time for Changes in Scenery**

If you're working on something that's particularly intellectually challenging, give yourself some time to transition between tasks. Set a 10-minute ringer and go for a 10-minute walk, a 10-minute yoga session, or a 10-minute tea session. Make the most of this time to prepare for the next task on your to-do list.

- **Organize Big Projects Into Smaller Tasks**

Adolescents and adults with ADHD often have difficulty focusing on multi-step projects due to the constant fear of being distracted. The key to successfully finishing large projects is to break them down into more minor phases that are easier to handle. Focusing just on the next attainable step can help you maintain your forward momentum. Make a sticky note of this step and put it somewhere where you can see it.

- **Make Due Dates Easily Recognized**

Make sure your deadlines are prominently displayed. You'll be reminded of the importance of maximizing your time. Adhesive notes on the wall above your desk or a laptop screensaver that says, "August 15 or Bust!" can help you stay on track.

- **Take a Brain Dump**

Writing down important tasks and dates in a calendar is a lifesaver for many persons with attention deficit hyperactivity disorder (ADHD). As soon as you're given an assignment, write it down in your planner. Otherwise, it will be overtaken by fresh ideas, facts, requests, or rumors. Organize your thoughts and appointments in a planner with plenty of "dumping" space. Also, don't ever leave the house without your planner. Ever!

13.3 WHAT TO DO WHEN YOU'RE FEELING OVERWHELMED AND EXHAUSTED

Your to-do list will catch up with you eventually, and you can't avoid it. With these methods, decluttering, resisting distractions, managing data, and getting things done can all be accomplished even from you.

- **Overcome the Overload**

Our days are filled with various stuff to keep us busy and occupied, including information, distractions, and our day jobs. It's not very surprising that anyone can't do everything they should, let alone individuals with ADHD or ADD. To keep up with the quick pace and constant interruptions, people with ADHD require some tactics for staying on track.

- **All That Data Must Be Recorded.**

You don't go crazy trying to remember everything that comes your way; instead, consider these solutions:

Record crucial information on your voicemail and leave messages for yourself. Voice recorder apps on smartphones can potentially be helpful in this situation.

Use apps like Google Keep and Evernote to convert vocal information into text.

- **Start Early Your Day and Complete Something, Anything At All**

When you conclude a task, whether it is minor or significant, you get a sense of accomplishment that helps you make the remainder of the day more meaningful. The fact that you can look back on the day and say that you accomplished something is motivation enough to keep on going the next day.

- **Make a Note of It and Schedule It**

Having a project on your to-do list isn't enough. It's a requirement that you must add it to your schedule. Setting a deadline for a task improves the likelihood of completing it. You have a 40% to 50% chance of completing a task if you solely use a to-do list—the odds of finishing the work rise by about 70% when you plan ahead.

- **Transform the Setting**

Women with attention deficit disorder (ADHD) can improve their ability to focus and concentrate by engaging in diverse tasks in varied environments. If you have to file your taxes, consider renting a hotel room for a few days. All of your paperwork and receipts can be laid out neatly, and there are fewer interruptions than there would be at home. When it's quiet in a library, some people with attention deficit disorder can't do anything—studying, writing, or reading. They will be more productive if they can find a place like a Starbucks where there is some background noise.

- **Don't Stress About Deadlines**

Allow yourself more time to complete a project. If you're unsure of how long each task will take, don't sweat it; just say, "Screw it. No matter what happens, I'm going to require at least 30% additional time to do what I've set out to do." Just randomly pick a number: 20% more, 50% more, and allocate that amount. The worst-case scenario is that you don't complete it ahead of schedule.

- **Chill and Carry On**

The first three things that cause you the most stress should be addressed first thing; after a good night's rest, the mind is calmer and more positive. People with ADHD are more prone to the internal deviation of worry that increases as the hours pass, making it difficult to complete tasks. So, three short morning steps in the right direction can help relieve your stress and allow you to get on with your life.

13.4 DAILY ROUTINE TIPS THAT WORK FOR WOMEN WITH ADHD

In addition to medicine and counseling, additional practices can help you organize your life if you have ADHD. The first step is to establish a habit and stick to it.

It will take patience, time, and customization to establish a reliable habit. Do you need some help getting started? I've put together a collection of nine tips for you.

- **Break Enormous Undertakings Into Smaller, More Manageable Jobs.**

Intimidating big, complicated projects can be overwhelming for those with attention deficit hyperactivity disorder (ADHD). Breaking down a project into smaller, more achievable tasks might help you get begun, keep going, and finish.

Instead of setting a time limit of three hours to finish a task, consider setting 25-minute targets and including them in your plan.

Consider striking out or marking off things that you've performed, even if they seem inconsequential. Even if it's only a modest gesture, it can make the remainder of your to-do list appear a little less overwhelming.

- **Create an Action Plan Before the Event.**

Prepare a list of everything you need to accomplish before you start a hectic day of tasks and work. Fix the most important things at the top of your to-do list first thing in the morning, when you're most likely to stay focused. Wait until the end of the day or a time of day when your energy levels are at their lowest to tackle smaller tasks.

Assuming you can accurately estimate the amount of time it will take, you will need to set aside more time than you think.

Writing and posting your schedule on a dry-erase board or large notepad is a good idea because it's easier for us to get sidetracked or derailed during the course of the day; as a result, you'll be able to keep your eyes on the schedule even when they start drifting off to other actions.

You'll also find it easier to stick to a schedule as you practice organizing your day and finding out how much time you need for each task.

- **Keep things simple.**

It's easy to get sucked into the temptation to overcomplicate things. But making a schedule too complicated for the sake of "perfection" is only going to cause more stress and anxiety.

Avoid adding unnecessary steps to your day. Make use of any shortcuts you may find to accomplish a task. Then, of course, you may cross it off the to-do list and move on.

- **Over time, develop a routine.**

In order to establish a habit, it will need some time. Health and productivity are both long-term goals that require patience.

One modest work at a time may be more manageable. Including dishwashing in your daily routine, for example, could help alleviate some of your tension. After doing the dishes every day for two weeks, consider adding another tedious task to your daily routine.

This way, you'll get into the habit of doing the things you don't want to do, and they'll become second nature.

- **Take some time for yourself.**

Taking time to relax, contemplate, and connect with others is essential. There is no one-size-fits-all definition of self-care, so do whatever it is that makes you happy and helps you unwind.

ADHD symptoms might worsen if you neglect your physical health, which can have a negative impact on your mental health. This can be lessened by scheduling meals and exercise into your daily schedule.

- **Set up distinct areas for work and play.**

"I don't have to get out of bed," we've all said at some point. "I can do this from bed too!" In particular, this has been made simple by quarantine and the ability to work remotely.

However, separating your professional and personal environments can help you be more productive at work and less stressed out while you're at home.

- **Incorporate sleep into your schedule.**

Women with ADD/ADHD are highly likely to suffer from sleep disorders such as insomnia and restlessness. Sleep deprivation or irregular sleep patterns can dramatically impact a person's daily functioning, emotions, and behavior.

Your schedule will be healthier and more regular if you include a good sleep routine and allow yourself enough time to rest.

13.5 PRODUCTIVITY ADVICE FOR ADHD BRAIN

Everyone swears by those best-selling productivity tips that are on the market today. For neurodiverse ADHD brains, they don't operate at all. Conventional advice may really be detrimental to your self-esteem as well as counterproductive.

Among the most popular productivity fads that I recommend you steer clear of:

"Eat That Frog!"
As we mentioned earlier, we should tackle the hardest thing to do first thing in the morning. But it is true that we have different levels of concentration and energy throughout the day, which this idea does not consider; in fact, this approach may be too much for those who are not too early risers.

A person's energy capacity can be divided into three distinct types of zones:

- The brilliant zone is the time of day when your mental abilities are at their highest, and you should focus on more challenging things. It's a state of great physical or mental energy in which your mind is racing at a mile per hour, and you're able to concentrate, but only for short periods of time.

- The dark zone is the time of day when you should be focusing on shorter, more interactive work because you will be distracted between different projects. This is the time when your energy is low, you are unable to focus, and you feel overwhelmed.

- Recharge zone. This may be the moment of the day when you're most likely to need a nap. Stretch, take a walk, or talk to someone for 15 to 20 minutes during this time.

Quick things first
If a to-do is faster, even if it comes out of the blue, this rule says to put it first; even if you know it won't have the most

significant impact and isn't the most important thing to do, gets rid of it now.

- A task that only takes a few minutes may actually take 15 to 20 minutes to complete because of ADHD's inability to accurately estimate and manage time.

- Then, remembering to pick up the previous task where you left off may be a bigger challenge.

The jar of stones
This strategy involves imagining your day as a jar of different stones: You put the larger rocks (the most important tasks) in the jar first, then the smaller ones (your less relevant tasks) should fill in the additional spaces, and finally, the remaining space should be filled with sand (quick/short chores).

- This technique assumes that doing the big value things first often equals success, which simply isn't true. If you push yourself to this kind of unattainable standard, you'll always feel like you're falling behind.

- It's not prioritizing the most important things that will make you successful, but rather doing the right thing for you first will!

Organizing Your Time
You can't manage time since it's out of your hands. The passage of time is a flexible concept. It's impossible to store or preserve in any way; you can never get it back.

- What you are able to control is how much time and effort you devote to a specific project. Your viability, not your schedule, should be your priority.

The To-Do List
To-do lists are not always the best approach to time

management. With an overly long to-do list may be easier to distract from vital chores. Also, not all jobs are equal. It's easy to get distracted from more time-sensitive jobs to complete simpler things like monitoring your voicemail or cleaning out your inbox.

- Instead of having a to-do list, organize your tasks into projects. Do some self-reflection: What are the most urgent tasks I need to complete? There are only seven items on that project list that haven't yet been completed. When you look at your tasks once a week, ask yourself, "What do I need to accomplish this week in order for this project to move forward?"

CHAPTER 14: ADHD AT WORK

A lot of challenges arise in the workplace for those who have untreated ADHD. The conflict between co-workers, delay, a lack of dependability, and a high error rate are all examples of interpersonal conflict. If these habits continue, reprimands, suspensions, demotions, salary cuts, and termination are all possible outcomes. In addition to increased unemployment levels and job-hopping, people with untreated ADHD often find it challenging to get hired for better-paying work.

Workflow Challenges

As a woman with ADHD, you must contend with extraordinary challenges and some limits of your mental faculties. As a result, you're more susceptible to feeling stressed or anxious; juggling all that is thrown at you might be more challenging.

- If possible, add more personnel to your team. Increase the amount of responsibility you delegate to your subordinates if you have any. Delegation is difficult for many people with ADHD, in part because it can produce a feeling of failure ("I should be capable of doing it all alone," for example). Work with them to set up processes that work, beginning with a timetable helping them to help you.

- Fix your priorities straight and stop trying to do it all at once. Develop the ability to say no, when needed. Ask for more time to complete chores.

- Keep a record of what happened. Whenever you feel overloaded, take a step back and consider what's bothering you. Some of your projects may have piled up because you believe you don't have enough time to complete them all. Consider breaking down big jobs into smaller, manageable sections of work. To help with this, you can create an outline.

Provide an overview of the project in one sentence or fewer.

1. First things first: what should I do?
2. What's the next logical step?
3. What's the cut-off date?
4. Who can assist me in taking on some of the responsibilities of this project?
5. What options does she have?

People with ADHD benefit from writing things down since it

relieves tension in their brains. Using a voice recorder to split down a task might also be beneficial for some people.

Phone Challenges
- Do you hate making phone calls? You can avoid this by making your calls early in the day and not thinking about them for a long time. Use a time when there isn't much going on in the morning to make calls that you hate and cross them off your list.

- Can someone at work relieve you of some of the phone conversations? In return for her taking some of the calls, you could perhaps trade tasks. Bartering chores can be a terrific solution when faced with a challenging task.

- If that's not an option, figure out precisely what it is about phone calls that irritate you. Is boredom an issue for you? Do you have a racing heart? Concerned about forgetting what you were going to say?

- To avoid becoming sidetracked when talking on the phone, try with a fidgeting spinner or draw on a bit of paper.

- Promote the use of email and text messaging as an alternative to phone calls.

Challenges with the Boss
- In many cases, workers feel overburdened when a superior issues orders or expectations in a "spitting" manner.

- If your supervisor does this, start carrying a notepad and taking notes when discussing new tasks, or ask her or him to jot down the basics of whatever you need to complete.

- Tell them that this is the greatest method for completing the task because it allows you to re-read the strategy.

Another great technique to deal with your boss's requests when your mind is already weary is to have him email you the task in detail.

Deadline Challenges

- For people with ADHD who procrastinate and leave projects to the last minute, create a calendar that breaks the project into sections and assign a specific day and time to each section. As a representation:

1. On Monday at 9 am, make calls to XYZ.
2. Work on one phase of your project for 1.5 hours.
3. Take a 10-minute break, take a walk, or think about whatever you want.
4. Return to the project for another 1.5 hours.
5. 12:30 pm: Time for lunch.
6. 1:30 pm: Do a review and report on your morning actions. Are you satisfied with your work accomplished?

Professionals on Board

- People who don't think they're up to the effort may find great relief in working with professionals who are experienced with the condition. You may benefit from engaging with an ADHD trainer who can assist you in setting up processes at work and hold you responsible for completing tasks. To work with your strengths, work with a coach.

- Another thing is to work with an expert organizer who can help you declutter your work. To avoid being judged, make sure the individual you hire is aware of the difficulties associated with ADHD.

14.1 16 ASPIRATIONAL JOBS FOR WOMEN WITH ADHD

Even while there isn't a perfect job for anyone with or without ADHD, a few occupations exploit and celebrate the abilities of women with ADHD more than others. These occupations help many women achieve their full potential by utilizing their natural talents.

1. Teacher

2. Journalist

3. Copy Editor

4. Food Industry Worker

5. Chef

6. Emergency First-Responders

7. Beautician

8. Small Business Owner

9. Hairstylist

10. Entrepreneur

11. Nurse

12. Theatrical Stage Manager

13. Software Developer

14. High-Tech Field

15. Artist

16. Daycare Worker

CHAPTER 15: STOP LOSING THINGS

Forgetfulness and ADHD, do you ever feel that your life is dominated by these two issues?? There are moments when I totally find myself unable to remember what I need to do or where I left my things. Where are my car keys? Where did I put my wallet down? What commitments did I have planned for today?

Even forgetting the smallest of details can be a hassle, if not aggravating. It's easy to forget small details that can have a significant impact on your day or week, just as ignoring key or important events can negatively affect your relationships.

As a sign of ADHD, forgetfulness can be a problem for both adults and children. Even Inattentiveness or an inability to organize one's thoughts might lead to forgetfulness.

I'm not telling you that ADHD and forgetfulness necessarily rule your day; we hope to provide you with a formula for dealing with them with more awareness with these tips.

Exercise Your Memory Using Memory Exercises
Memory exercises can be a fantastic way to combat the symptoms of ADHD and forgetfulness; they are an excellent way to keep your mind occupied. They are also valuable reference points from which to draw your memories.

- Thanks to the help of visual aids such as a picture or sketch, you can help your brain remember what you've just seen or done. Instead of relying on your own recollection, you can use the drawing for jogging your memory and recalling whatever you need to remember from it.

To Stay on Top of Things, Utilize Calendars and Reminders

Learning how the ADHD brain works is critical to treating forgetfulness due to ADHD. With ADHD, many things can be difficult or problematic to remember.

- Take advantage of technology-based calendars and reminders to help overcome unavoidable difficulties. Electronic or printed calendars, such as those provided by your email provider, can be a great way to keep track of future events and appointments. There are also electronic calendars with built-in reminders.

Inform Your Peers

Sometimes you may feel that your forgetfulness and ADHD are a burden you can't lift. You may not want to burden people with your amnesia because you don't want them to feel uncomfortable around you.

- When you talk to others about your forgetfulness and ADHD, you might ask them to help you remember things you might otherwise forget. The fact that you tend to forget things sometimes is exceptional to admit to your friends and colleagues, I know, but you don't need to be embarrassed with them. Talking about it honestly with them will give your work life a positive boost, and you'll feel a lot of gratitude for them.

Take a Deep Breath and Relax

When you're under much pressure, you're more likely to make mistakes and get distracted. As if you weren't already overloaded. On the other hand, stress might exacerbate the symptoms of ADHD and forgetfulness.

- Chronic stress has been shown to impair memory. Anxiety and memory are both mental processes, so it's only natural that they'd interact; to avoid becoming overworked, make sure to spend time away from your work to recharge your batteries.

- Try the strategies in this chapter to de-stress your day to boost both your memory and overall well-being.

Acknowledge Your Limits

No one can do it all; everyone has their own setbacks! For many persons with ADHD, forgetfulness is not the only barrier to face on a daily basis. But instead of rejecting your constraints, you should accept them and use them to your advantage.

- In order to overcome ADHD and forgetfulness, you must first understand that you will never have a perfect memory; there will always be a time and place for big or small forgetfulness.

CHAPTER 16: SAVE YOUR FOCUS

"How come I can't concentrate?" You've long known that good intentions don't always convert into concentration, especially when the task at hand is tedious, demanding, or time-sensitive.

12 WAYS TO STAY FOCUSED THROUGHOUT THE DAY

These 12 ADHD-friendly tactics will help you build the attentional patterns you need to focus on for long periods of time.

1-Make sure to keep in mind the Zeigarnik Effect
According to the "Zeigarnik Effect," tasks that have been started but not completed are harder to remove from your memory. This means that even if you only work on a project for 10 minutes, your brain will have a more challenging time forgetting or discarding it. Once started, a daunting task will become unfinished work, and subconsciously, your mind will continually turn to it for guidance on how to complete it.

2-Build your "parking lot."
ADHD minds can easily become distracted by racing thoughts, from laundry or answering Aunt Linda's phone calls. A "parking lot" is a convenient place to store unwanted thoughts until they can be addressed at a more appropriate time. A notebook in your bag or a corner on your desk for post-it can act as a parking lot for you, allowing you to focus on your current task without distraction better.

3-You can use a "daily focus list" to help you keep track of your priorities.
Prepare a list of your top priorities daily and refer to it throughout the day. Use it to shut out annoying distractions and refocus at regular intervals! "To-do" lists aren't just a way to keep track of what needs to be done. They're also an anchor tool that helps you keep your focus on the most essential things in your life.

4-Do not just follow the crowd.
Hyperfocus, for example, is one of ADHD's many superpowers, but you can't always predict when it will manifest. Respect

your intellect!!! Acknowledging the difference between being "in the zone" and being "foggy" is just as vital as knowing when you're in the latter state. Doing less strenuous duties like filing paperwork or folding socks is perfectly acceptable when you're entirely zonked out. Your productivity will increase in the long term!

5-Find out what causes you to feel overwhelmed.
Stress triggers the ADHD brain's fight-or-flight response. A lack of ambition appears to be the cause of this: You give up on your mountains of housework or unfinished tax returns in favor of binge-watching Netflix. Begin by recognizing the things that make you feel overwhelmed, and then take steps to avoid them. There is a large range of reasons why some people are unable to focus on their goals. Finding out what triggers your overload isn't going to stop it from happening every time, but you'll be able to better predict its approach and plan accordingly.

6-Forget about perfection.
While hyperfocus can be beneficial, the pursuit of perfection is not. It can lead persons with ADHD to worry over minor, inconsequential details—and in the process, sabotage their ability to focus on more essential tasks. Let go of your need for perfection and accept that "good enough" is good enough. Don't assume your perfectionist traits to go away overnight, but you may expect to lessen your stress, boost your self-esteem, and enhance your efficiency as you go down the path.

7-Distract yourself with happy distractions.
A word like "distraction" doesn't have to be dirt. In some ways, some distractions can even help you get more done. I know it may seem contradictory to take a break from work to get some exercise, but it's actually good for your mental health and can help you return to work more focused.

Meditation, a short music break, or an art activity are all examples of "positive distractions." Set a few minutes for your positive distractions in your daily routine and stick to those minutes; set a timer if you're worried about getting lost in your distraction.

8-Set aside some time to plan.
When you don't know what you're supposed to be doing exactly, it's hard to keep focused on the task at hand. A minute of preparing can save you 40 minutes of effort. Therefore, it's crucial to schedule small planning sessions to outline goals and deadlines for upcoming days or weeks. No matter if priorities can change and crises can happen, nothing is set in stone. You can get back on track by having a rough idea of what you want and how you'll go about achieving it, even when things go awry.

9-Become part of a team.
Be sure to work with an "accountability partner" who will keep track of your progress and help you celebrate your victories on a regular basis. This is a win-win situation for anyone, especially those with attention deficit disorder (ADHD). In order to reach your goals, you need someone to lean on—it could be an ADHD therapist, a family member, or even a friend.

10-Set a timetable.
Have you ever wondered why you always put everything off until the last possible moment? Your ADHD brain, always on the go, needs deadlines. And it's easier for the brain to focus on and complete a task with specific deadlines because deadlines reduce competing priorities and increase adrenaline. When a task doesn't have a clear deadline, you need to set one yourself.

11-Answers to your questions.

Clarity makes it easier to stay on task and accomplish your goals. In order to figure out what's causing your disinterest in a task, ask yourself these questions: What are you hoping to accomplish? This project is being driven by your very own or someone else's expectations. Do you know what you're supposed to be doing? Ensuring you know what you're expected to do will help you avoid distractions and keep a pleasant attitude.

12-Recognize your negative thoughts.

Remembrance is the greatest opponent of focus and productivity. It is virtually impossible to function if you constantly think about a recent disagreement with your spouse. On the other hand, negative ideas can be avoided by adequately recognizing them. Don't be afraid to acknowledge your habitual thought patterns; set up a time when you can do so and benefit from the process. To keep your focus, say to yourself, "I know that last night's disagreement upset me and that my current feelings are valid, but I have decided to move on and not be distracted by it."

CHAPTER 17: STOP PROCRASTINATION

WHERE DOES MY PROCRASTINATION COME FROM?

Procrastinators, as we know, regularly avoid complex tasks. They put off commitments at work, at home, and in their relationships; these bad habits negatively affect their productivity and quality of life in every area.

Awareness is the first step to overcoming procrastination.

Here are some excuses and their solutions to identify and stop your procrastination habit:

"I Can Do It Tomorrow"

When you're exhausted or stressed, it's easy to put things off until later; as a result, you may not have the amount of time you expected to complete all of your tasks before the end of the day.

You might think about putting them off until the next day. But while this may be possible today, it may not be possible tomorrow. Every day there may be unforeseen events that you can't foresee, and you know that even your best-laid plans can fall apart because of one small setback.

Solution:

If you find yourself putting things off, sit down and think about what you need to do in the future. Write down a specific time to do the activity, so you won't forget about it when the time comes. Make an oath to yourself that you won't be excited to do it the next day if you're postponing it off because you don't feel like doing it today.

"I don't need to document it."

"I will definitely remember this" or a variation of this are common expressions for those with ADHD. As a result, you often neglect necessary actions, such as keeping track of important information that should be remembered and added to your to-do list. I understand that keeping a journal is frustrating and time-consuming. But being called back down to earth every time something falls into oblivion (again) is an even bigger hassle.

Solution:

Documenting and repeating to yourself what you should be doing will help keep you from forgetting, so consciously remind yourself that minor inconveniences due to your procrastination could lead to major difficulties down the road. Remember how good it will feel to clear the next task rather than how horrible it will be if something goes wrong later.

"I can do anything in a matter of seconds."

For people with ADHD, it's tempting to prioritize quick things before moving on to more challenging tasks. What's the big deal? It will only take a minute. Sending one email contributes to reading another, which leads to visit a link, and so on. The difficulty arises when you overestimate the value of that short action and underestimate the impact it will have on your productivity. Believe me, you'll end up spending time you don't have, which is not a good thing.

Solution:

Ask yourself how prone you are to getting caught up in lesser things before praising yourself for being efficient. Which are the tasks you would be able to get out of in a matter of seconds if you were trapped in a multitude of activities? Recognize them and avoid them, especially if you are in a hurry!!

"I think I'll be able to stay up a little longer."

After a long working day, you may have the desire to stay up late and have some fun or watch a lot of shows on TV, simply because tomorrow morning's problems don't exist tonight.

Or the purpose of staying up a little longer before going to bed is to finish the work that was left undone from the previous day.

The result doesn't change; the next day, you'll be so tired that you'll easily procrastinate on most of your tasks.

Solution:

The amount of sleep you need is a matter of personal preference, so be honest with yourself. Think about how hard it will be to get out of bed the following day and how long and agonizing it will be the next day. Staying up "just a little longer" is a temptation that should not be indulged.

17.1 TIPS FOR BREAKING PROCRASTINATION

1. Make the most of your time. Get a stopwatch, set it for ten minutes, and get to work. See what happens if you put all your efforts into that short period of time.

2. Use your anxiety as a tool to your advantage. Stressing a little about looming deadlines has the added benefit of clearing your head of distractions and excuses. "When time is of the essence, you're able to think outside the box and come up with new solutions.

3. Get help from a friend. Encouragement from a friend or partner is sometimes all you need to inspire you to take action. Someone you appreciate and admire who has your back can help you keep your commitments to yourself and your goals on track.

'You can do this,' she'll tell you. 'You'll feel better once you take care of this,' she'll say to you again when your urge to procrastinate gets the best of you.

4. Remind yourself of what's essential. For the vast majority of individuals, to-do lists are a helpful tool if they are used correctly. Use sticky notes, computer notifications, or any other software that serves as a reminder.

5. Overcome self-doubt. Procrastinating on an important task can have a dramatic effect on your emotions, as well as the explanations you give yourself. Don't torment yourself; lift your head and move forward even when you're feeling down.

6. Organize work into small parts. Is there a project you haven't been able to get started on? It's best to break it down into a series of small tasks that you can complete and finally strike it off your to-do list. As a result, you'll feel a sense of accomplishment and be motivated to tackle the next item on your list.

7. Set a goal of finishing a project as quickly as possible.
Incorporate your ability to perform well under pressure into your planning. Use the metaphorical eleventh hour to know how close you are to meeting your deadline in advance.

CHAPTER 18: HOW TO PRIORITIZE

FIND OUT WHAT'S MOST IMPORTANT TO YOU

Most women with attention deficit hyperactivity disorder (ADHD) wander through various daily activities without much thought, not really knowing which of these activities can positively impact their days. They also often follow the suggestion to write a priority list, but how many of them stick to it? Even many end up putting it in a place where it will never be discovered.

Learn how to prioritize and get it down on paper if you really want to stop being controlled by your ADHD. You might ask yourself, how do I actually use the list every day with so many requests, chores, and interruptions? Is there any way my list can help me complete my tasks?

Some suggestions:

- For your priority list to be effective, you need to review it often. First thing every morning, I recommend setting a reminder to review your to-do list to cross them off as soon as possible.

- A brief mental review of your priorities may keep you from taking an interest in new ideas, requests, and tasks. If they are not urgent, you will put them on the back burner; however, this does not imply that you will not attempt them. To overcome the temptation to do that task before focusing on matters that do have priority, you will need to become adept at the art of scheduling your activities and not deviating from them.

- Remember to make your ADHD self-care routines a priority as well that keep your ability to focus. It's easy to ignore them, but believe me, it's also very risky. Take care of your brain so that it can take care of you.

- Re-Check your list of priorities at least once a week to make sure they're still relevant. Make sure your goals are aligned by scheduling weekly planning sessions. It doesn't have to be a long and tedious process; while you're doing it think more about how beneficial it will be in terms of time saved!

CHAPTER 19: TIME MANAGEMENT

When it comes to time management, adults with attention deficit disorder (ADHD) have a unique perspective. Great procrastination and the inability to organize and complete our tasks on time contribute to our deadlines, timeliness, and scheduling difficulties.

There are several ways actually to meet your deadlines. Isn't that encouraging? With these time management tips in mind, you'll be able to meet any temporal deadline, no matter how daunting it may seem.

The first step is to post your deadlines in a prominent place where you can always see them. It will remind you of the relevance of maximizing your time.

Don't try to do too many things at once.
Plan ahead based on the amount of time you have available in your hectic schedule. To meet the deadline of an important task, you may have to agree to reduce the amount of time you spend on other actions.

Change your inner voice.
Hang in there by saying encouraging things to yourself. Writing "positive affirmations" is a practice I sometimes do to engage myself.

Set deadlines for yourself and others.
Our hatred of deadlines is so great that we are often unwilling to set reasonable deadlines for others either. My teachers were often willing to answer my questions while I was working on my thesis. But if they didn't respond by Friday afternoon, I would have to wait until Monday morning to start, which irritated me greatly. As a result, I would lose

focus or justify that I couldn't continue working because I was uncertain what to do next.

Work on small projects and set a deadline for each one.
Most of the time, we are given a deadline to complete the project. If you want to stay on track, set time goals yourself, such as finishing a quarter of the project by Thursday and so on. These dates will help you identify potential problems before they get out of hand.

Identify your goals.
At first, my goal was to study everything I could about my topic; once I felt convinced, I would move on to the next step. But it wasn't until I decided to finish my studies by the end of March that I was able to focus on the hard part, the writing. For people with ADHD, among the most desired goals is being able to complete tasks on time.

Take breaks frequently.
Those who refuse to take a break from a project are more likely to give up or abandon the undertaking altogether. When I didn't feel like taking a break, I would ask my co-worker to force me to do so. This was what often kept me from becoming overworked.

When you're short on time, delegate.
I took a lot of time putting the finishing touches on my research. It was time to send the project to an editor, which I did. An entire day's work was saved as a result of this.

Don't assume that every part of a project is your responsibility. In many circumstances, outsourcing or delegating makes sense.

Start and finish on time.
I worked every day from 8 a.m. to 5 p.m. while writing my

research, allowing me to socialize in the evening. I was able to keep going since I knew I would finish at 5 p.m. For example, I would repeat to myself, "Only two more hours until 5... one more hour." I probably would have abandoned my writing many times by mid-afternoon if I hadn't defined stopping at 5 p.m.

19.1 9 RULES TO SAVE YOUR TIME

Understanding ADHD traits, such as inattention and/or impulsivity, is critical to effective time management. You can learn to better manage your time by changing some of your habits and your routines. Rules to allow you to set clear boundaries and learn how to respect them are mentioned below:

Two minutes rule.
Do this thing now, or within two minutes. You know you can't believe yourself if you try to convince yourself that you will do it later. When we promise ourselves to do something right away but don't, not only are we wasting "bandwidth" in our brains, but we know that we will forget about it within a few minutes.

In the future, when you have forgotten the plumber's name, you will thank yourself for doing something as simple as immediately capturing and tagging the contact in your phone! "One stitch in time saves nine," as my wise grandmother used to tell me when I was younger.

Don't be afraid to say no.
Saying "no" when you would usually say "yes" can be awkward at first, but with practice, it gets easier. Practice answering, "Let me check my schedule to see if this is something I can fit in" when someone asks if you can do something for them.

A timer can be a helpful tool.
You can set a timer if you are hyperfocused and lose sight of time, resulting in lateness or missed appointments.

Set a limit and make it clear.
Set a time limit for monitoring email, Twitter, Facebook, and newsfeeds, and stick to it. A winning rule of thumb is to limit social media use to lunchtime or the journey home from

work. Delete any app with an alert icon from your home screen if you don't want to be bothered by it. Unsubscribe from unnecessary emails, newsletters, and organizations that waste your time only.

The hidden dangers of multitasking.
To benefit from multitasking, you need to be very focused and organized. Doing one task at a time will save you time, especially when the tasks are new and complicated. It's okay to help your kids with the calculation problems while cooking the same meal you've made a hundred times, but if you're trying out a new recipe and assisting your child with the math, you'll see more than likely burn through dinner, and your child will fail the test.

Learn to Delegate
Let go of the idea that "If I want it done well, I must do it myself, since showing others how to do it will make me lose more time," and instead focus on how to delegate the task. Make time to teach others and be gentle with yourself. The long-term benefits are substantial.

Expend twice as long
In many cases, adults with attention deficit disorder (ADHD) have a hard time anticipating how long something will take. As a result, organizing needs a great deal of making a judgment, and many of us might get bogged down in basic issues like "Keep or toss?"

Don't accept interruptions when you're in the midst of anything.
The time you're wasting isn't the fault of your kids, your job, or social media. You may not realize that some "good" behaviors are actually sabotaging you.

Get rid of these unhealthy behaviors that are keeping you from achieving your goals, stealing your time, and just

causing you stress:
- Don't accept anything less than perfection
- Trying to complete all tasks at all costs
- Don't engage in necessary (but painful) activities
- Attempt to solve all problems immediately
- Ignore your long-term goals
- Aim for universal acceptance
- Respond promptly to all calls, texts, or emails
- Never stop working

CHAPTER 20: ADHD THERAPIES OVERVIEW

Many women seek therapy for attention deficit hyperactivity disorder (ADHD) because they have difficulty managing their finances, time, employment, and family responsibilities. On the other hand, other women are more adept at concealing their symptoms, working late into the night, and attempting to "order" their lives in their spare time. Women typically express themselves as feeling stressed and exhausted regardless of whether their lives are in a state of disarray or they can keep their problems hidden.

20.1 9 MOST EFFECTIVE THERAPIES FOR ADULTS AND CHILDREN WITH ADHD

ADHD medication and behavioral therapy are proven to be the most effective treatments for children, especially those who demonstrate oppositional conduct. Adolescents with ADHD still benefit from therapy even as they get older. Many adults use ADHD counseling to learn social, behavioral, and intellectual knowledge that will enable them to manage their symptoms throughout their lives.

Consult an ADHD expert to help you or your child select which kind of therapy is most suited, and utilize the summary below to grasp the nine most prominent therapies for AD/HD.

1. Cognitive-Behavioral Therapy

Behavioral treatment aims to improve children's behavior with attention deficit hyperactivity disorder (ADHD) by establishing routines, developing predictability, and providing positive attention at school. Common-sense parenting is the first step toward a successful behavioral therapy plan. Behavioral interventions for ADHD should include the following:

- Use a reward system to encourage positive conduct.
- Negative behavior should be ignored and discouraged.
- Take away a perk if the negative behavior is so severe that it cannot be tolerated.
- Eliminate typical causes for negative behavior.

Practicing CBT, adults work with a therapist who assists you in identifying and changing your bad habits in order to get better results from this treatment. Cognitive-behavioral therapy (CBT) is a brief, goal-oriented style of psychotherapy to alter the ADHD negative thought patterns, the way you perceive yourself, your talents, and your future. Here's the breakdown:

- Focus on one issue behavior at a time, such as procrastination.
- Identify and modify the beliefs and perceptions that lead to the behavior.
- Find realistic approaches to alter the behavior
- If the strategies don't work, try something else.

2. Neurofeedback (also known as brain training)

Brain exercises are used in Neurofeedback to help adults and children with ADHD control their impulsiveness and focus their attention. Neurofeedback treats ADHD signs like distractibility, impulsivity, and outbursts. It teaches the brain to produce thought patterns associated with concentration, not daydreaming.

According to a computer's analysis of brain activity, ADHD symptoms may be traced to sections of the brain that are overactive or underactive. Neurofeedback claim to improve focus and cognitive ability without the need for medication. There is still skepticism among the scientific community.

3. ADHD Coaching

Children, adolescents, and grownups with ADHD can benefit from the assistance of ADHD coaches. Coaches can assist children in developing intellectual and emotional growth, learn effective learning methodologies, and achieve strong social skills, business exploration, and intelligent financial planning.

Even adults with ADHD face many obstacles, and an ADHD coach can assist them in learning how to overcome those difficulties. A coach can be a taskmaster or a personal assistant.

- Structure your life in a way that makes sense to you.
- Become and remain inspired
- Promote business exploration and intelligent financial planning.

- Learn how to better handle your time and money

The ADHD Coaches Association is one of the most excellent areas to find an ADHD trainer. Here it's possible to find resources for both coaches and those in need.

4. DBT: A Dialectical Approach

Dialectical Behavioral Therapy (DBT) and Cognitive Behavioral Therapy (CBT) target the social and emotional difficulties that come with disorders like ADHD and others. Emotional control has become one of the most excellent effective treatments. In weekly group sessions, DBT is presented in a sequence of skill-based modules, each one focusing on a specific ability. Individual therapists offer further assistance in tailoring the application of these abilities in real-world scenarios.

5. Music Therapy

Music therapy helps people with ADHD improve their focus and concentration, lessen their hyperactivity, and improve social skills.

Music shapes the moment. An ADHD brain's struggle to remain on a linear route can be soothed by the rhythmic structure of music.

Synapses are activated by music. Even dopamine levels in mind are increased by listening to enjoyable music. Working memory, attention, and motivation are all affected by a deficiency of this neurotransmitter in ADHD brains.

Music is a social activity. Tomaino, a 40-year veteran of music therapy, advises: "Think of an orchestra. You can't play the composition if one of the instruments is absent." There is no substitute for all voices.

6. Play therapy

To assist children with ADHD to interact, learn, provide reassurance, calm anxiety, and increase self-esteem through play therapy. Play as a therapeutic tool allows therapists to influence children's thoughts, feelings, and actions in a non-direct manner. "Children communicate figuratively through play," explains Houston-based child psychologist Carol Brady, Ph.D. It's like providing a sweet medication rather than a bitter one" as a therapeutic technique." An essential part of bonding with a child is playing with him/her.

7. Art Therapy

Adults and children with ADHD, and other neuropsychological problems, benefit from art therapy because they are better able to express their feelings visually and artistically than verbally or in writing. Art therapy can be particularly beneficial for women with ADHD because it keeps their arms moving and creates an intense emotional and mental attention that is not often attained in talk therapy.

8. Equine Therapy

Equines are used in Equine Assisted Psychotherapy (EAP) as a form of interactive ADHD therapy in which clients engage with horses instead of talking about their issues.

ADHD can be treated using Natural Lifemanship, an EAP methodology. A trauma-informed strategy based on neurobiology and the importance of healthy, linked relationships is the foundation of this method. To develop a bond with a horse, clients learn to control their body energy & pick up on nonverbal cues. For example, the horse delivers instantaneous and direct responses to the human's activities that people cannot or will not.

9. Nature Therapy

Taking a walk in the trees or spending time in nature frequently may help alleviate symptoms of ADHD.

Many professionals recommend nature therapy, along with prescription drugs and behavioral treatment.

20.2 BEST ADHD TREATMENTS FOR WOMEN

Adult women with ADHD are best treated with a multimodal strategy, which includes a variety of complementary treatments. The best combination may consist of medicine, nutrition, physical activity, and cognitive behavioral therapy, among other things. Taking vitamins, constantly engaging in CBT, and attending an ADHD support network may be optimal options.

1. Medication

For one simple reason, research suggests that medication is the most effective first line of defense against the signs of ADHD, but drugs aren't an excellent size-fits-all solution.

Patients need to consider the following things before beginning pharmaceutical treatment:

- Some people have adverse side effects from medications. It takes many trials to find a medication regimen that strikes the right balance between side effects and benefits; it also brings many tries to find the best medication and dosage for you.

- Finding the proper drug, dosage, and schedule can take months.

- For the best results from medicine, you must talk with your doctor and execute his/her instructions, especially during the first few weeks of treatment. This exchange of information is essential for prompt dosage adjustment and adverse effect management.

Studies have indicated that combining medication with behavioral treatment and/or coaching is more beneficial to managing ADHD.

Keep in mind that adopting only medication is not the solution; ADHD symptoms can be alleviated, but the disorder cannot be cured.

2. Behavioral Therapies

For most women with ADHD, experimenting with multiple therapies is critical to achieving desired outcomes. And it's crucial for those trying to balance their personal and professional lives. Behavioral therapy focuses on specific problematic attitudes and helps the patient learn new ways to deal with them to improve various areas of life. A common strategy of behavioral therapy is "conditioning," which is used to influence behaviors and includes the following:

- Encouraging the appropriate action in a particular situation

- Providing positive reward and feedback for proper behavior and improvement

- Withholding reward or appreciation or enforcing negative consequences are examples of direct repercussions for unacceptable action.

Asserting that one's actions have positive and negative effects is crucial. Behavioral therapy has a positive impact on many people's undesirable habits and behaviors.

3. Exercise

Exercising activates the attention system, known as the "executive functions," such as sequencing and working memory.

The benefits of only 30 minutes of walking four times a week are astounding. There is no doubt that more intense exercise has more advantages for your brain and body, but the point is clear: Always get moving!

4. Supplements and Nutrition

ADHD-friendly nutrients like iron, zinc, fish oil, and

magnesium, as well as protein and complex carbs, can improve the brain's ability to function and lessen mood swings.

5. Yoga and Mindful Meditation
It's crucial to pay attention to your feelings, thoughts, and sensations in order to build a broader awareness of what's going on in your life at any given time. Yoga can be used to improve physical and mental health, lower blood pressure, alleviate chronic pain and anxiety.

6. Couple Therapy
Many women with ADHD benefit from couples and family therapy by working with loved ones to develop effective behavior plans, boost accountability and cooperation, and enhance interpersonal communication and relationships.

20.3 NINE INNOVATIVE OPTIONS

An ADHD mind is wired differently than a neurotypical brain, and most people who care for or work with someone who has ADHD don't know how to deal with it in a way that works. They chastise the individual (or parent) if the therapy doesn't work and demand that he re-tries it. Affirmations like "You're lazy!" or "You didn't really try" convey that the individual didn't succeed because of a personal problem. However, it's the treatment that's flawed, not the individual.

These are 9 different approaches to treating ADHD:

- **Find a Cheerleader**

Having an unwavering belief that you are intelligent, reasonable, and caring is the most essential factor in achieving success and happiness in life. As a child, the most accomplished people with ADHD had a father, brother, teacher, or even a sports coach who loved, supported, and respected them. The primary key of a cheerleader is to discern between a child's worth and his accomplishments. Who said adult women shouldn't have a cheerleader too? Find your "person" who will support you and push you to always be your best.

- **With ACT, You'll Get Things Done.**

Doing what your boss believes is essential or meeting a deadline doesn't drive persons with ADHD. In the absence of positive reinforcement, Acceptance and Commitment Therapy, ACT, aids a person with ADHD to maintain concentration and stay motivated throughout the day. ACT encourages women to think about the most important things to them, such as family, home organization, getting ahead at work, or having confidence in God. Women in the ACT program must ask themselves, "Am I accomplishing the most important thing to me?" Meds can be taken to create a level playing field.

- **When You're Not Interested, Make situation Interesting**

To access their strengths, people with ADHD have to build interest where there is none.

A medical student with ADHD was failing anatomy. Since Kennedy was his idol and solely motivation to finish medical studies, his ADHD coach made him believe he was the emergency room doctor who had treated President Kennedy after he was shot. To save Kennedy's life, he had to be competent in anatomy. The student was promoted to anatomy and graduated second in his class by exploiting the motivation of this perceived urgency.

- **Assemble Your ADHD Toolbox**

Always carry a pen and small planner with you, keep a record of things that have worked for you or your kid that have brought you this far. Consider the times when you're engaged, productive, and energized when you're in the "brilliant zone." How long ago was it? What threw you out of your comfort zone, and what helped you get back on track? Month by month, you'll be familiar with several tactics that you can use when procrastinating.

- **At College, Take the Wheel**

Young women with attention deficit disorder often find themselves in the position of having to make things more exciting themselves. If there are 5 English classes to pick, look for the brightest and most entertaining instructor. Ask pupils what they think in the classroom and take the class that you are most interested in taking.

- **Find a Push to Keep You on Track**

Tutors often employ the body-doubling approach, but it can also benefit those with ADHD in the workplace.

A lawyer with ADHD was fed up with missing deadlines because of his inability to plan ahead. He got his helper to bring him 1 case at a time, clearing his desk of any distractions. They talked about planning what he every day needed to do, and she made sure he was taking care of himself as well.

- **Formatting Modifications**

People with attention deficit disorder (ADHD) frequently find it challenging to communicate their knowledge to others. So, they must come up with new ways to show off their abilities.

When a student with ADHD had difficulty writing in English class, he sought help from his teacher. He found the assigned reading tedious. Rather than doing book reports, he talked to his teacher and persuaded her to create parodies of the novels. He aced all of his English homework and was awarded the top prize.

- **To Prevent Boredom, Inspire Competition**

Women with attention deficit disorder (ADHD) are able to swiftly grasp new jobs and interests, only to lose confidence in them. You may benefit from a little bit of a challenge. Many people with attention deficit disorder (ADHD) enjoy the challenge of trying to beat their own personal best or a competitor or imagine the job as a computer game in which you must progress to the next level.

- **Organize the cards to your advantage**

As long as the woman's motivation is not involved in the process, ADHD therapy is likely to fail. The desire and your ability to see the benefits of treatment will be used to reinforce goal attainment. Subsequently, the treatments and therapies adopted will give you an advantage over the symptoms.

You will soon realize that you have all the cards you need to win the challenge!

CHAPTER 21: ADHD WOMEN FAQ

21.1 FREQUENTLY ASKED QUESTIONS FOR WOMEN WITH ADHD

● **Question:**
Is it possible to lead a successful life if you have ADHD?

Answer:
ADHD is a challenging condition, but there are both pros and cons. It is possible to overcome the challenges and live a fulfilled life by relying on widely available resources, skills and methods.

● **Question:**
Isn't ADHD medicine just another form of illegal drug?

Answer:
No, medical prescription stimulants, on the other hand, are safe and effective therapies for people with ADHD. However, it is crucial to keep an eye on patients about indicators of abuse and dependence.

● **Question:**
What are the pros and cons of telling my co-workers or employer that I have attention deficit hyperactivity disorder?

Answer:
A co-worker may be more likely to help you with specific tasks if you disclose that you have ADHD. Talking openly about your difficulties with someone you trust and spend a lot of time with, such as a co-worker, often proves a win-win solution.

A potential employer may be more likely to not hire you or attempt to fire you if you disclose that you have ADHD. Adjustments and legal protections cannot be made if the information is not made public.

● **Question:**
Can it be harmful to people with ADHD to spend too much time on the computer or other electronic devices?

Answer:
Computer screens can be physically, intellectually, and emotionally stressful for long periods of time, whether the content is engaging or boring. It's a good thing to know that there are multiple simples to use and readily available strategies that can help.

- **Question:**
Isn't ADHD simply an excuse for laziness?

Answer:
A lack of ambition or the appearance of lethargy may seem like a sign of ADHD, but it's not. The underlying cause that makes people with ADHD lazy and listless is actually a problem of neurological processes in the brain. There's nothing you can do about it! It's not a lack of personal ambition!

- **Question:**
Are there supplements that can help alleviate the symptoms of attention deficit hyperactivity disorder (ADHD)?

Answer:
The use of single nutrients to treat ADHD has not been successful, except with omega-3 fatty acids. Combining dosages of minerals and vitamins has proven to be more effective than any single supplement in the long term. In this book, you will find the ideal supplement solutions to your condition.

- **Question:**
What is the link between emotional control and ADHD?

Answer:
In addition to impulsive emotions, ADHD is associated with various mood and anxiety disorders. However, the emotional responses of those with ADHD may be more fleeting or sometimes more evident, depending on the context in which they manifest. DESR and impulsivity (EI) in ADHD can separate difficulties and impairments in social interaction from mood disorders.

- **Question:**

With ADHD, which are methods to lessen the burden of stress?

Answer:
People with ADHD have more possibility to be overweight, and the risk increases as they get older. Often, they are also more likely to suffer from eating disorders such as anorexia and bulimia—especially women with ADHD.

- **Question:**

What's the connection between ADHD and weight gain habits?

Answer:
People with ADHD have more possibility to be overweight, and the risk increases as they get older. They are often more likely to suffer from eating disorders such as anorexia and bulimia—especially women with ADHD. One of the leading causes is that those who are living with ADHD have circadian rhythms thrown off; there is no stable balance in their daily routines, so eating habits are also affected. Also, having with increased dopamine activation in the reward area of the brain, they are more likely to overeat and, as a result, be obese.

- **Question:**

What dietary changes should people with ADHD make?

Answer:
One of the main reasons people with ADHD consume unhealthy foods, even though they are aware of the dangers, is that their impulsivity is highly influenced. They often fall victim to advertising that makes junk food most attractive and convenient. A possible remedy for not giving in to harmful temptations may be to make a list of healthy foods for meal

preparation, stick to it carefully and go to the supermarket only if you are on a full stomach after eating a meal.

● **Question:**
What is the significance of diagnosing and treating ADHD in adulthood?

Answer:
ADHD can be diagnosed and treated even in adulthood; it's never too late to improve your life, and you can't treat a problem if you don't know what you're dealing with in the first place. An accurate diagnosis of attention deficit hyperactivity disorder can be performed at any age. Coupled with proper treatment, make the difference toward self-acceptance and effective symptoms care.

● **Question:**
When one partner has ADHD, what are the most typical relationship issues?

Answer:
Anger-related conflicts are more likely in a relationship where one or both partners have unmanaged attention deficit hyperactivity disorder. Shame, caused by a sense of inadequacy, can also be a debilitating condition for women with ADHD in their relationships, but it doesn't have to be. With the right emotion management tactics, you can go a long way!

21.2 PROFESSIONALS' ANSWERS TO THE TOP TEN QUESTIONS ABOUT ADHD IN WOMEN

After being diagnosed with ADHD, many women have so much more questions than answers. So, what's the best course of action? How can I describe my condition, attention deficit hyperactivity disorder? How can I acquire good specific habits for my job or education? Here are the answers to your 10 most pressing post-diagnosis questions from professionals.

1. Why wasn't I diagnosed with ADHD sooner?

ADHD is no longer regarded as a "childhood" disorder. Since 2014, more adults than children or adolescents have been diagnosed with ADHD. At this point, the average age of diagnosis has risen to the mid-30s. The reasons for this change are several.

- Only a tiny percentage of kids with ADHD are obviously hyperactive. Thus, the illness is typically overlooked.

- As a result, ADHD is commonly misdiagnosed because it has both good and negative characteristics. People with ADHD have a unique ability to think outside the box and develop creative solutions to problems. "Cognitive dynamism" is the current word. When persons with ADHD "get in the zone," they have a persistent desire and get engrossed in the work they have discovered to be so fascinating, even though they are easily distracted.

- It was no longer necessary for diagnosis to include hyperactivity when the condition's name was modified to highlight inattention. Girls were as likely to be diagnosed with ADHD, and the condition often lasted into adulthood.

2. **How can I know whether the ADHD medicine is working for me?" Exactly how long would it take to see results?**

Monitoring the effects of the medicine on the individual's target symptoms is one of the most excellent ways to measure a person's improvement while taking ADHD medication: These are the signs and symptoms that impact a person's day-to-day activities.

- A slight and brief loss of appetite may occur due to an increase in dosage, although this is the only side effect to be expected. The dosage can be adjusted each week in order to lower the possibility of adverse effects.

- The dose can be increased more quickly in late teenagers and adults since they are more aware of their reaction to medication and can express it more clearly. When the proper dosage is achieved, no further improvement will be shown at a certain point.

- At that point, the dosage found is ideal, as it manifests itself in peak performance with no unwanted side effects.

3. **Besides taking stimulant medication, what other therapy alternatives are available to me?**

- ADHD disorders and their level of impairment can affect the severity of symptoms. While medication is probably the primary treatment for ADHD, there are other options for treating mild to moderate symptoms even without medication.

- The **first step** is improving focus, emotional self-regulation, and executive functions through parent training, skill training, psychotherapy, or coaching.

- The **second step** is addressing the underlying causes of the symptoms.

- In order to keep your brain healthy, the second thing you should do is adopt a better lifestyle. Enhance your sleep quality, eat a healthy diet, supplement with micronutrients, exercise, and cultivate mindfulness.

4. **What are the immediate and long-term negative effects of ADHD medication?**

Overstimulation is the most prevalent short-term adverse effect. People experience agitation, headaches, a lack of appetite, and difficulty sleeping as a result of the stimulant. Similarly, a person loses all desire to do anything, their facial expressions become expressionless, and they appear emotionless. These side effects may be alleviated by reducing the stimulant dosage or utilizing a different stimulant.

5. **Can I pass ADHD on to my child?**

About 50% of women with ADHD seem to have inherited it" Doctors at the National Institute of Mental Health say at least half of all parents who had ADHD in their youth have children with the disorder.

Many parents only become aware of their ADHD after one of their children has been diagnosed with ADHD. Think of the problematic implications this can have: an impulsive, highly constrained, hyperactive child raised by an impulsive, unstructured, distracted mother who was probably not diagnosed with ADHD.

6. **How can I describe ADHD to my newly diagnosed child?**

It can be tough to convey to your child that he has ADHD. Many parents are unfamiliar with the science and specifics of ADHD, which makes this discussion a little more complicated.

It's important to think about the dialogue from your child's perspective. We don't know what's on his mind. What is she going to be concerned about? In the long run, your child's mindset will be influenced by this. When addressing ADHD with your child, use these talking points:

- It's going to be a period of time before this is finished. But I'll be there for you every step of the way.

- That's great! A couple of the issues that have plagued us in recent months have been resolved.

- We're already in love with you as you are. The person you are will not be altered in any way. You'll be the better version of yourself possible.

- You likely got your ADHD from me. Therefore, we're all going to learn about it together.

- There may be medications that can help you. Try them, and let's evaluate together whether they can have a positive impact on your life.

- I'm not going to sugarcoat it: it's sure that you're going to have to put in more effort in school or at work than the others.

- It's fine to have a different perspective than most of your pals, as long as you keep it in perspective. You're not broken or injured in any way. At times, it's hard to believe that you're better than anyone else in the room.

Remember that regardless of your child's age, the way in which you talk to them about something is probably more essential than the substance of what you tell them.

7. How can I receive an Individualized Education Program (IEP) for my child?

A doctor's note is not enough to secure an Individualized Education Plan (IEP) for your child. Let your child's school know-how and that ADHD affects their academic progress.

If your child has some difficulties in school or behavioral problems in the classroom, it's critical to be able to eliminate other possible causes, such as typical learning problems.

Talk to your child's principal or counselor and urge that the school conduct an evaluation of your child's attention and learning issues. An assessment can help you, and the school determines if your child is experiencing difficulties in the classroom.

Suppose your child's problems are extreme or relatively mild. In that case, whether they're limited to attention or include learning difficulties, whether they can be helped only with accommodations or require specialized instructional support, the assessment will help you and the school comprehend how best to help your child succeed.

The Individuals with Difficulties Education Act (IDEA) may be necessary for students with severe ADHD and learning disabilities. To be eligible for special education services under this federal statute must be identified as having a handicap.

8. How much control does my kid with ADHD have over his or her own actions?"

Several things influence a child's behavior, including their level of mental growth, the prevalence of developmental disorders such as ADHD, and the circumstances that motivate them.

So, it's clear that children can exercise some degree of control over their actions depending on their age and circumstances, and that's a fact. For children with ADHD, a deficit in self-regulation, the behavioral difficulties are more significant. Psychologists recommend parent training programs and school management measures to improve a child's behavior.

9. What are the long-term consequences of ADHD?

The long-term consequences of ADHD are influenced by a

wide range of circumstances such as a person's health status, family life, friendships, and education.

With ADHD, there is no single outcome. Although they have problems with inattention, restlessness, and difficulty with interpersonal relationships, many children or adolescents with ADHD can do well in school, their families, and their social circles when they become young adults. Often, during coaching, we meet youth with ADHD who are able to lead happy and successful lives.

Adult women with attention deficit disorder may be deeply dissatisfied with unfinished things, become depressed, and have low self-esteem.

When ADHD is not diagnosed until well into adulthood, getting a proper diagnosis and treatment can make a big difference in its long-term impact. There are now countless methodologies available to combat ADHD that will allow you to live happily and with dignity.

10. What is the link between emotional control and ADHD?

In addition to impulsive emotions, ADHD is associated with a variety of mood and anxiety disorders. However, the emotional responses of those with ADHD are more fleeting, triggered, and particular to the context in which they occur. DESR and impulsiveness (EI) in ADHD can help separate social interaction difficulties and impairments from mood disorders.

CONCLUSION

To conclude this long series of tips, techniques, and strategies, I would like to tell you that I know the difficulties you are going through and have gone through, often alone, because no one knew what ailed you, not even you.

I know because I've been there myself.

Remember, it is essential to consult a professional if you suspect you have attention deficit hyperactivity disorder. An appropriate diagnosis and treatment strategy will help you get relief from your difficulties and significantly improve your quality of life. Talk to a psychiatrist or your doctor about your symptoms for a more accurate diagnosis.

Health professionals have a greater understanding of the various behavioral patterns of ADHD in girls, adolescents, and women to identify specific indicators of the disorder, treat them early, and preserve women's mental health.

At any stage of your life, whether you're of reproductive age or menopausal, it's critical to keep ADHD symptoms under control. Communicate your condition to your gynecologist as well. You need to understand that it is vital to learn all you can about ADHD and the symptoms that can negatively impact every area of your life, take note of the medications you are taking and achieve all the help you need.

When it comes to ADHD in young women, there is a lack of awareness, and the reasons for this remain a mystery. As a result, ADHD involves a good deal of insecurity, low self-esteem, and shame, making social relationships very difficult.

It frequently happens that after learning that one of her children has been diagnosed with ADHD, many mothers realize that they have the same condition. After learning more about her child's ADHD symptoms, the mother notices many of the same patterns in her own behavior. The difficulties increase exponentially when both parent and child have the ADHD disorder; in this case, it is of the utmost importance to begin family therapy immediately.

If you have ADHD, you know how frustrating it can be to have trouble concentrating, getting things done that you need to do, and keeping track of your daily tasks. Setting and maintaining a schedule can be a valuable strategy in managing the more adverse symptoms of ADHD.

Learning to manage the intense emotions you feel and your continued distraction will allow you to succeed in every area important to you.

As a woman with ADHD, in this book, I've collected for you the best strategies and tips I've implemented myself to cope with my condition, and sometimes, by circumventing the difficulties, I've gotten great results from them.

My sincerest wishes go out to you, dear reader, with the hope that you will soon find the awareness you need to deal with ADHD; only then you will reach your full potential and live a life as fulfilling as any other woman's.

I am grateful to you for choosing this book and trusting me. I hope you found the help you were looking for to overcome the challenges of ADHD and that these contents will help you thrive!

Janet O' Wild

Printed in Great Britain
by Amazon